GIVE US THIS DAY

A MEMOIR OF FAMILY AND EXILE

GIVE US THIS DAY

A MEMOIR OF FAMILY AND EXILE

Helena Wiśniewska Brow

Victoria University Press

TE WHARE WĀNANGA O TE ŪPOKO O TE IKA A MĀUI

VICTORIA
UNIVERSITY OF WELLINGTON

VICTORIA UNIVERSITY PRESS
Victoria University of Wellington
PO Box 600 Wellington
vup.victoria.ac.nz

National Library of New Zealand Cataloguing-in-Publication Data

Wiśniewska Brow, Helena.
Give us this day : a memoir of family and exile / Helena Wiśniewska Brow.
ISBN 9781776560509
1. Wiśniewski, Stefan. 2. Wiśniewska Brow, Helena.
3. Refugee children—Poland—Biography. 4. Refugee children—
New Zealand—Biography. 5. World War, 1939-1945—Refugees—Poland.
6. World War, 1939-1945—Refugees—New Zealand. I. Title.
305.906914092—dc 23

Printed in China by 1010 Printing International

To my parents—Stefan and Olga Wiśniewski

Author's Note

The geographical and historical breadth of this story means that it crosses many boundaries of language and place. Polish, in particular, can appear daunting on the page to English-speaking readers, while shifting borders and political regimes in Eastern Europe and Central Asia over the last century have meant that many place names have changed, sometimes more than once. The following notes explain why I have used particular names and spellings, and clarify instances of Polish pronunciation.

Place names

Where possible, I have used place names appropriate to the story's chronology in this text. For example, the pre-war Polish town of Brześć becomes Brest following its Soviet takeover in 1940. Similarly, particularly in Central Asia and Iran, I've generally used the place names and spellings that my father was familiar with at the time—though many of these have since officially changed. In some cases, hazy and traumatic childhood memories have complicated this process; some places remain necessarily nameless.

Personal names

Poles use informal diminutive first names among friends. Different diminutives have different emotional connotations, ranging from neutrally friendly to strongly affectionate. The Polish family members and friends in this book are named as I knew them—for example, my uncle was never Kazimierz to me, but the less formal and more friendly Kazik, just as my aunt was always Hela, never Helena. Surname endings, similarly, sometimes differ to indicate gender. Wiśniewski, for example, is the nominative form for a male in my family; Wiśniew*ska* is the form for a female. Some female family members now living in New Zealand, however, have chosen to simplify matters by using the male nominative form only.

Pronunciation

Polish pronunciation is not as difficult as it looks and follows regular rules (for example, emphasis is almost always on the penultimate syllable). But for the occasionally complex-sounding names and words used in this text, here are some phonetic soundings and, where appropriate, English meanings.

Alicja/Alina—*ah-leets-yah / ah-leen-ah*
Basia—*bah-shah*
Czesław/Czesiek—*ches-wahf / ches-shek*
Izabela/Iza—*ee-zah-bellah / ee-zah*
Jozef—*yuw-zef*
Kazimierz/Kazik—*kah-zheem-yesh / kah-zhick*
Marysia—*mah-ri-shah*
Regina/Renia—*re-gee-nah, ren-yah*
Wacek—*vaht-sek*
Wiśniewski/Wiśniewska—*vish-nyev-ski / vish-nyev-skah*
Wojtek—*voi-tek*
Zbigniew—*zbeeg-nyef*

Brześć—*bzhests*
Kraków—*krah-koov*
Wrocław—*vroh-swahf*

Ciocia—Aunty, *choh-chah*
Dziadzio—Grandad, *jah-joh*
Dzień dobry—hello, *jen-dob-ree*
Dziękuje—thank you, *jen-koo-yeh*

SWEDEN

BALTIC SEA

Riga

Gdańsk

Szczecin

Wilno

1945 border

POLAND

Poznań

Wisła R.

Bug R.

Warszawa

Brześć

Warta R.

Dobrynka
Piszczac

SOVIET UNION

Łódź

Wrocław

Lublin

Prague

1945 border

Kraków

Lwów

CZECHOSLOVAKIA

CARPATHIAN MOUNTAINS

Stanisławów

Vienna

RIA

Budapest

HUNGARY

ROMANIA

250   500 km

Gained: Territory annexed
by Poland in 1945

Lost: Territory annexed
by Soviet Union in 1945

Map 1: Poland's territorial losses and gains, 1945
Wiśniewski family home, pre-World War II: Brześć and surrounds

(Maps by Geographx Ltd)

Map 2: **Wiśniewski family deportation and exile, 1941–1944**
Soviet-occupied Poland to Siberia, 1941
Siberia to Iran (probable route), 1941–1942
Pahlevi to Esfahan, Iran, 1942–1944
Zam family home, pre-Russian revolution: Feodosiya, Crimean peninsular

This place where you are right now,
God circled on a map for you.

Hafiz

Prologue

Neither of them is looking at the camera.

Hela, my father's sister, stands behind the makeshift wooden crucifix, a cotton scarf tied under her chin. In Mary Jane shoes and white ankle socks, she doesn't look her 19 years. Next to her, my father, 14-year-old Stefan, is bare-kneed and in oversized shorts. His eyes, lowered, are fixed on the fresh and dusty grave at his feet.

It's June 1944, and the grave is my grandmother's. A week before this photograph was taken, 49-year-old Stefania Wiśniewska was buried without ceremony in the Polish corner of Tehran's Catholic cemetery. These two children, the only family members then aware of her death, had travelled north from the Iranian city of Esfahan in the back of a canvas-topped army truck to say a belated goodbye. For Stefan, who'd had no idea his adored mother was so sick, no idea she'd even come to Tehran for surgery, this evidence, a heaped mound of recently turned rubble, is scarcely believable.

The photograph of their visit is a black-and-white souvenir of his bewilderment. Today it sits in an album with yellowed pages, some of them empty, that my father keeps in an old-fashioned suitcase with flick-up clips. He has few photographs of his early years, certainly none from before the war, so this is perhaps the youngest image of him I will see, probably the saddest.

Here is the end of your mother, it says. Here is the end of your world.

~

Dad has to bend to put his case of photographs away, his square fingers fumbling with the low cupboard handle. It seems I'm interested in the kind of detail that he either can't or won't recall. Who arranged the truck for them? Who took the photo? How long did they stay in Tehran? He can't remember any of those things, he says.

'You know, I ended up in hospital the day after this photo. I had malaria,' he tells me. 'When I got off the truck back in Esfahan I didn't know where I was. I hardly remember being at the cemetery that day.'

I'm asking because I've never seen this image before. Not much more than a year ago, I stood with him at that same grave in Tehran's eastern suburbs, just as his older sister once did. The cemetery looked different when I was there, of course. The dust and rubble had been tidied away under blankets of concrete and strips of grass. The old brick walls that still lined the cemetery's perimeter, separating its Catholic foreignness from the rest of that Muslim city, were hidden behind veils of green foliage. Maybe that's the way my father prefers to remember his mother's death, I think: the rawness gone, a loss smoothed by time. Maybe it's just me who sees it as a terrible turning point in the movie of his life, time rewinding like a clacking reel of film, frame by frame, back to that graveside vignette. My grandmother's death sent the lives of her children, lives already way off course, spinning in an even less familiar direction. For my father it was a trajectory that would end here, 70 years later, in a country on the wrong side of the world, in a carpeted townhouse in a city of foreigners.

My father puts his glasses back on his nose, sits down in the tub chair under the window, sighs and looks at me.

'So, where to next do you think?' he asks. 'We haven't been to Siberia yet. After Iran, Siberia will be easy.'

There's a pause as he studies my face.

'Okay, I'm keen if you are,' I say. 'That would be great.'

He looks tired today. His skin is as rough as his fleecy top; his eyelids are puffy. He's well enough, though, for a man who's about to turn 84. We both know he would clear his almost empty calendar for a journey to Siberia, the only stretch of his story that we haven't yet retraced.

'What would that one be?' he asks. 'Our fifth?'

I've never counted. I know our first trip together was in 1988, when he was only a few years older than I am now. Since then we've been to Poland a number of times, to Belarus, and now to Iran. Each journey has started the same way: retracing roads that he remembers and people whom he mourns. I've followed his lead, attempting to make sense of the tangled snatches of stories I heard as a child. But I'm not sure what our shared journeys have achieved. They've simplified nothing and clarified very little; they have created new stories of ours to add to old stories of his. We have to reminisce about our changing travelling companions because everything else is so muddled. Do you remember 1997, we'll say, when Mum came to Poland with James and Anna? When we put five candles on Anna's cake in our Warsaw hotel room? And what about 2009, when the Canadian schoolteacher with the glasses was so kind to us in Gdansk? What happened to him?

A trip to Siberia's vast wastelands may be overdue—I'm not sure why that place has always felt so out of reach for me—but I know there are no easy answers waiting there for us. And I find it difficult to believe, even now, that my father would willingly revisit his first place of exile. So we take measure of each other's seriousness: he knows I am unsure; I know he is too. We are also both aware, but don't say aloud, that a trip to Siberia would take months to set in motion, maybe longer. Would he be strong enough to cope with the rigours of even a post-Stalin Russia? There's Mum to think about: she couldn't come with us, but could we leave her? And how would I get away again? Would

James want to come? My sister? The children? I'm surprised by how panicked this thinking suddenly makes me feel, the understanding that perhaps we are reaching the end of our travelling, my father and I. I'm surprised at the way my throat tightens.

'Let's do it,' I say. 'Let's go to Siberia next year.'

But then Mum comes downstairs to say goodbye, descending slowly and almost sideways on the narrow stairs. She places one hand and then the next on the wooden bannister, each movement a small, deliberate act of bravery. My white-haired father and I watch in silence. Time is running out for the stories—his, hers and ours. They are racing, too fast, to their conclusions.

1

I'm a poor audience for my memory.
She wants me to attend to her voice non-stop,
But I fidget, fuss,
Listen and don't,
Step out, come back, then leave again.

Wisława Szymborska, 'Hard Life with Memory'

In May 1988, I stood on a Polish riverbank with my father and my uncle, looking at the Soviet Union. The grassy banks opposite stretched away in either direction, ending in lazy curves, one turning left, the other right, before disappearing from view. There was nothing to see beyond the murky water and the tree-covered banks: only an open early summer sky, white lumps of cloud.

'So this is it? The Bug River?' I asked.

'No, the Bug River,' my father said. 'Bug like in boogie.' He stretched the vowel, exaggerating it with pursed lips. 'It's the border. Just over there, that's Brześć, where we lived, that way, not far. If we could get across, we could walk from here.'

I know that, I was ready to say. I know all about this town, about this river; I grew up with these names lodged in my head like unwelcome visitors. I was teasing with my silly English joke. But my father wasn't looking at me. He'd turned to his brother.

'Why didn't we get a visa, Kazik?' he said. 'We should have got a visa, so we could go home and look. I can't believe we didn't get a visa.'

I stared at them. What did he mean? We had travelled as far east as we could and this sleepy river was the end of the line. Behind us was our car, its doors open to the afternoon heat and buzzing midges. I could hear my Polish uncle Wacek and his wife Jasia chatting in its back seat, waiting for us. But my father's aquiline profile was still fixed eastwards, his eyes scanning the Russian riverbank as if willing the past to emerge from behind a clump of reed. Kazik, a darker, rounder version of his middle-aged brother, was staring too, shading his face with his hands as he looked. Somewhere out of sight and out of reach was Brześć, the pre-war Polish town that had once been their childhood home and that was now the Russian town of Brest.

The Poland we had been visiting, Poland in 1988, was a country desperately kicking its way out of the Soviet Union's grip. Its faded cities, empty shops and sad, drab population were more than the slow-burning legacy of 50 years of Soviet domination. In the early 80s, Poland had also suffered three years of martial law; the crippled economy those years produced had sent hundreds of thousands of Poles fleeing for the west. I thought it was depressing. The rural charm of these open borderlands with their endless horizons and swaying birch trees was lost on me. Our shiny leased Renault had marked us out as strangers and the novelty of being stared at and chased by excited children when we slowed through narrow village lanes had long worn off. I'd had enough of visiting bathroom-less cottages owned by distant relatives wearing headscarves. I was tired of feeling out of place. I wanted to go home.

Home for me at the time was London. I'd been there almost two years, happily employed in the cramped Fleet Street office of the New Zealand Press Association, writing stories for the newspapers at home on football hooligans, Antipodean businessmen, retail trends and royalty gossip. It was fun. I was 25 years old and—I had to keep pinching myself—making a living doing something I liked in a city that I had once only dreamed of visiting.

'Things always fall into place for you,' my Wellington flatmate had said to me with surprising bitterness when I told him I'd been offered the job. 'You're just a lucky person.' I knew it was a great opportunity for a rookie journalist. But there was something about being reminded aloud of my good fortune that had made me uncomfortable. I'd carried his words to London with me in my suitcase like a bad omen. So far, everything had been fine, but standing there on the banks of a river in eastern Poland, I felt them work their way into my head again. I was lucky I didn't have a Russian visa, I thought. I was lucky that I didn't have to go there.

Waiting for me in London was also the boyfriend who'd encouraged me to do this trip with my father. 'You might not get another chance,' he had said. 'You should go.' James and I shared a room in an attic flat near Wandsworth Common and when we weren't working took cheap and romantic long weekends in European capitals and went to country pubs for lunches on winter Sundays. We partied as often as we could with other noisy Kiwis in bars and restaurants in the King's Road and Covent Garden. Our aim (wasn't it everyone's?) was to have as much fun as possible. So I can only just remember my middle-aged father arriving at Heathrow airport from Auckland with his brother, both men still slim and brown-haired, years stretching ahead of them. I can't remember clearly what tempted me to join them on a four-week, figure-eight loop of Poland. I recall only my fears. How would I cope with my first taste of Soviet-style communism? More scarily, how would I cope with these aged travelling companions?

Maybe it helped that my father had held his tongue about my new domestic arrangements in London. Unsurprisingly, he'd declined my half-hearted offer of a bed at our flat, booking instead an over-priced Bloomsbury hotel room that he shared with his brother. When he did visit us, climbing the three storeys of staircase to our front door, he seemed impressed. He avoided glancing at the bedroom but chatted happily to James over tea at the kitchen table, admiring the botanic prints inherited from the previous tenant on our cream walls. I knew, of course, that Dad wasn't as comfortable as he looked. Mum had already warned me. 'Don't tell your father I've called,' she'd said. But I hadn't anticipated his tactful silence. Perhaps my very Catholic father had finally noticed that I'd spent the previous two years creating a new, more grown-up version of myself.

I was wrong. My father's silence didn't indicate a shift in the tectonic plates of our relationship. He had simply—perhaps under pressure from my more practical mother—made a decision to hold his tongue. In hindsight, it was a clever move, letting me feel like an adult: I must have decided it was time I paid my father and his story some attention. I'd spent my childhood trying to ignore the past my father obsessed about, a homesickness that he seemed unable to let go. I'd never understood what it was about the comfort and safety of life in New Zealand—and, it seemed by implication, my mother, my sister and me—that had always failed to satisfy him. Maybe, for the first time, I realised there was something I needed to know.

We left London in the rain on 10 May. The grey waters of the English Channel, viewed through the hovercraft ferry's foggy windows, reflected my gloom. Even the shiny blue Renault my father had leased at bargain rates in Calais, the most up-to-date car I'd ever driven, didn't cheer me. Later that night, in a hotel room somewhere off the autobahn outside Hanover, I must have opened my journal for the first time. I only just recognise myself in its neat, sloping handwriting. 'S & K seem a little lost at the moment . . . I hope they snap out of it!' I wrote, in text overloaded with exclamation marks and adjectives. In Poland two days later, Wrocław's cobbled streets and its pastel-coloured architecture fail to get a mention and the tone of my writing is still inexplicably whiny. 'Something is very wrong here. If it wasn't for the kids and the sunshine it could be quite depressing! I wonder what we will do for a *whole* month!'

Wrocław was where we were staying for a while; it was home to Polish relatives I had never met before. I remember the jolt I felt when I met my Uncle Wacek for the first time. He was an older, sharper-featured replica of Dad and his heavily hooded eyes were an eerie blue version of my own. Wacek and Jasia lived in a small but spotless flat on the third floor of an inner-city block. This was the seedy Milan Kundera communist backdrop I'd always imagined and secretly feared: its stairwells, lined with graffiti, smelt of something unpleasant (could it be urine?) and led to streets of empty shops and blank-eyed people. There was little for sale in the supermarkets, certainly nothing familiar or appetising to me, and long quiet queues snaked out of dimly lit shop doorways. But in the evening, generous meals—rich soups, meat, vegetables, fruit compotes and yeasty poppy seed cakes—somehow appeared from Jasia's cupboard-sized kitchen. The food was delicious.

Wacek and Jasia had three children, all grown, but it was their son, my older cousin Wojtek, who became my unofficial caretaker. He was a secondary school teacher with a scarily Slavic moustache and he spoke—luckily for me in this household of Poles—careful English. Within days my cousin had arranged a clandestine exchange of US dollars for cans of petrol and rolls of Polish złoty in a garage near his apartment. Maybe, I belatedly realised, he was the family member who had arranged the provisions for his mother's menus. Wojtek and his wife Beata, a doctor, had two blond daughters, the youngest of whom seemed to spend most days in her grandparents' tiny flat while her mother worked. I played with three-year-old Kasia—

my lack of Polish didn't bother her; she was happy to take my hand and chatter—while Wojtek watched. He seemed amused by our childish interaction, but I found his scrutiny unnerving. I wondered what he thought of me in my London jeans and silly, shiny lipstick.

Benek, another of Dad's older brothers, was unwell and undergoing treatment for the cancer that would later kill him. We visited him one afternoon in Wrocław's main hospital. I remember Benek's grey face and the sadness of the men in the ward who watched our family reunion from their beds. I don't remember anything else. 'Was very glad to get out of that hospital,' my journal tells me now, a permanent and shameful record of my youthful selfishness. 'It stank of sick people. Six men crammed into a stark square room. And sauerkraut for afternoon tea!!'

From Wrocław, we took the car to Warsaw, with its strange and Disney-like old town, and Kraków, glamorous but drooping. And then we went east, as close as we could get to my father's birthplace without a visa, to stand on the banks of a river and look across the murky water to where he really wanted to be.

∼

We didn't go to Russia on that trip. I drove our shiny Renault west, back to the sparkle and safety of London, of my boyfriend and my job. My father and my uncle returned to New Zealand.

I wasn't aware then that I had visited Poland at a turning point in its history. It would never again be the traumatised and angry place I remembered. Poland had begun its transition from satellite Soviet state to democracy and two years later would hold its first post-communist free presidential election. Many of the people I met in 1988—people who fed me, gave up their beds for me, nudged me to marry, grow my hair, put on weight—would not be there the next time I was. But even as my life resumed, I knew something had shifted. I couldn't forget my father's ease in a country that was so foreign to me, his face and his voice finally like everyone else's. Dad was looking for something in Poland and I didn't know what. I wanted to be there when he found it.

~

Every time my birth is discussed, my father tells the same story.

'When I got to the hospital after work, that's when I saw you,' he says, as if this is the only logical place for his story to start. I've given up asking how my young father, his fingernails still dirty from the pulp and paper mill, could happily make such a late arrival at Whakatane Maternity Annexe on that afternoon in March 1962. Things were different then, I'm always told.

'Anyway, this nurse,' he says, 'she just put a baby in my arms like a parcel and said, "Here you go." And so I take a look at this baby and I get such a fright.' He has shifted to the present tense. He mimes holding a newborn in the crook of his bent arm, an awkward new father peering at his daughter's face for the first time. Then he looks up and grins at me, his grown-up daughter, who is still listening because she likes the story and the way it makes her father so animated.

'I just said to the nurse, "Oh no, I'm sorry, but you've made a big mistake, this baby's not mine." And then I tried to give the baby back to her.' My father always laughs at this point, delighted.

'Ha! So funny! I thought you were Chinese!'

It may have been as simple as the colour of my eyes: like my mother's, mine are dark brown. My father had never known a brown-eyed blood relative, and his dark-eyed daughter would have been a shock. Perhaps, though, he saw something else. Perhaps it was a centuries-old genetic echo, a spooky reminder of one of the Crimean Tartar or earlier Mongol invasions of the rich lands that separated Europe and Asia. But all of my family history, maternal or paternal, is untraceable beyond a generation or two. For my father, it's a history that starts and ends with his parents.

His mother, my grandmother, is spoken of with such respect by those who loved her—my father, his siblings, those who believe they owe their wartime survival to her—that the little that is known about her barely does justice to the scale of her legacy. There's certainly very little about Stefania that's tangible to me. Her pleasures, her sense of humour, the way she walked, her habits: all are mysteries. If my father is asked about her he speaks in generalisations, of her admirable qualities. Of course, Stefania must also have once been someone's fresh-faced daughter, probably someone's annoying sister, as well as my father and his siblings' adored and brave mother. But no one remembers the names or faces of her family. All that's known is that when my grandfather wed the blue-eyed girl with the heart-shaped face from Międzyrzec Podlaski, north of Lublin, he 'married up'. Stefania Ostapowicz was 15 years his junior and from a family of some social standing. Józef, my grandfather, of whom more is known, was from humble stock.

$\sim$

Józef Wiśniewski's family worked a small farm on the flatlands in Dobrynka, close to today's Polish-Belarusian border. There were six Wiśniewski children, but it was Józef's younger brother, Franek, who was to become the farmer. My grandfather, born in 1880, was more ambitious. He was a railway man, a role with some status in the days when unemployment was high and steady government jobs, particularly in eastern Poland, were sought after. He and his new wife lived what would prove to be a critical 40 kilometres south east of the Wiśniewski family land, across the River Bug, in a small railway house. The house sat on a plot close to the short stretch of branch line for which Józef was responsible, its tracks running south from the nearby city of Brześć. The family's home, the place where their 11 children would be born, was in the newly re-Polonised lands of the Kresy, the eastern borderlands of Poland.

The Kresy region, like the long-demolished family house, is unmarked on any map of Eastern Europe today. But its historical outline roughly straddles the three borders of Western Ukraine, Western Belarus and Lithuania. The Polish perspective of the Kresy is often a romantic one: it is the country's cultural heart, its historic and traditional homeland. But the Kresy has also been the focus of centuries of violent push and pull between the neighbours who have laid claim to it. In the 1700s, Poland was partitioned three times by the expansionist states of Russia, Austria and Prussia, with the last of these partitions, in 1795, effectively wiping Poland off the map. The low-lying grasslands and ancient forests of the eastern borderlands were then annexed to Russia and were regarded after that—perhaps critically—as Poland's 'stolen lands'. In 1918, at the end of World War I, when it became clear that Poland would become an independent country again, the Kresy was in the spotlight. Between 1918 and 1921, the new Polish state fought three wars with the Ukraine, Lithuania and Russia to re-establish its eastern borders, eventually successfully annexing the region.

The new Poland viewed its redefined eastern border as a restoration, not an annexation. It was an opportunity to civilise and progress a region that had been neglected and impoverished by successive wars and poor government: in 1918, it was believed that 40 percent of the Kresy's population of mostly rural peasants were illiterate. After 1921, Polish state and government structures were installed, as well as new schools and compulsory primary education. New Polish military settlers, often landlords, replaced former Ukrainian and Belarusian owners. This 'Polonisation' was, unsurprisingly, welcomed by few of the existing inhabitants of the Kresy. Many Belarusians resented the Poles as occupiers; many Lithuanians to the north and Ukrainians to the south were similarly aggrieved. Polish–Belarusian, Polish–Ukrainian and Polish–Lithuanian conflicts and skirmishes were common between the wars.

Caught between these cultural conflicts was the region's already geographically and culturally isolated Jewish population. More than 1,000,000 of Poland's then 3,000,000 Jews lived in the Kresy, most of them unassimilated, Yiddish-speaking. My father remembers that while some were impoverished, the majority were 'reasonably well off, at least compared to us'. The Jews were the merchants, lawyers, doctors and craftsmen he remembers, the people who supplied services and goods to the less educated and poorer Poles. My grandparents, he believes, regarded their successful Jewish neighbours with a mixture of envy and resentment. This post-World War I Kresy, with its underlying political and cultural currents, was a precarious and complex society in which to raise a family. Despite these uncertainties, and perhaps because of the fervour and vibrancy of Polish nationalism that characterised these years, the Wiśniewski children grew up in a Poland they remember only as idyllic.

~

I give my father a piece of paper and a pencil.

'Draw your house for me. What did it look like?'

He draws a large rectangle, tentatively, and looks at me, as if awaiting my opinion. I realise I've never seen him draw anything before. 'It was just a big room,' he says, apologetic. 'Very simple.'

It was made of rough sawn timber, and built in a traditional rural Polish style. The family cooked, slept and lived in the one central room, with provisions and other household items stored in an annexe, all of it under one pitched, tiled roof. Water was carried in from the well, lighting came from candles or kerosene lamps, bread was baked in the wood oven that also served as their winter heating source. In the colder months, my father remembers, cotton wool was stuffed between the panes of the double-thickness windows for extra insulation. The lack of view was no problem; there was nothing to see outside but snow. They kept several pigs for meat and two cows for milk, grew their own vegetables—potatoes, cucumbers—and hay for the animals. In autumn, they collected mushrooms from the forests and in summer, berries. The only foodstuffs bought from the shops at the local Jewish village, Wołynka, were the things they couldn't make or grow themselves, luxuries like sugar and salt.

The Wiśniewski family was poor, he says. Not unusually so among the ethnic Poles of Brześć, but poor all the same.

One family photograph taken in 1916 is a formal studio portrait of a serious group, each participant dressed in best clothes. In the centre is Józef, a stern and dark-haired man, his small face overshadowed by a heavy, black moustache; behind him and to his left is Franek, his brother, a man with a broad-shouldered farmer's body in military uniform. On Józef's right, and slightly out of focus as she juggles a baby on her knee, is a round-faced Stefania in a dark dress with a girlish, white Peter Pan collar. The baby, in a smock, is Florian, my father's oldest brother. If I ask my father about the other women and children in the photograph, each of the latter awkwardly clutching unfamiliar toys, he can't tell me for sure. They could be Franek's wife and family, or they could be Józef and Franek's sisters. This vagueness isn't strange: my father's memories of his childhood include nothing of Józef and Stefania's respective families. No grandparents visited the house, he says, although it's clear that

31

Józef's mother, at least, was living with Franek only a short distance west across the Bug River during his childhood. My father does remember one visit from an aunt, a woman in smart clothes he understood to be from his mother's well-to-do side of the family. On one other occasion, a man—he assumes his uncle, Franek—arrived on a horse and cart loaded with vegetables for the family's winter stores. But the Wiśniewski family was a self-contained and tight unit on the whole; there was little time, energy or money for fun.

After Florian, the family grew at an astonishing rate. Bernard (Benek) was the second son, followed by Wacław (Wacek) in 1920. In 1922, Regina (Renia) was born, the first Wiśniewski daughter, followed by Helena (Hela), then Roman (Romek) and Czesław (Czesiek). My father, Stefan, was born in 1929, then his brother, Kazimierz (Kazik) and finally two sisters, the youngest just before the war: Izabela (Iza) and Alicja (Alina). The size of the Wiśniewski household meant life was never easy, especially for his mother. My father claims to remember Stefania distinctly from those years, though again he finds it difficult to give a physical description. She was an 'intense' person, he says, focused on managing the home and ensuring her children had the education they needed to raise them from their 'working class' lives. His mother's educational ambition for her children, rigidly policed by his disciplinarian father, defines his memories of his childhood.

'All the money we had went to education for my older brothers and sisters,' he says, 'all of it. I think my parents saw it as the only way to get ahead.' He recalls how proud Józef and Stefania were of their two older sons, Florian and Benek, both of whom graduated as engineers shortly before the war. The younger children walked the short distance to school in all weathers without complaint. The primary school they attended was new, probably one of the public institutions hastily created

Wiśniewski family, Dobrynka, 1916: Stefania (left) with baby Florian, Jozef, seated (centre) and Franek, in uniform (top right).
If I ask my father about the other women and children in the photograph, he shrugs. They could be Franek's wife and family, or they could be Jozef and Franek's sisters.

Fourteen-year-old Hela, in Brześć, Poland, 1939.

by the Polish government in the post-war fervour of Polonisation to educate the country's new periphery.

'We had hooks to hold our coats,' Dad remembers. 'And they gave us slippers to wear inside so we wouldn't mark the new floor. We had a great time sliding around.'

Children from Brześć's different ethnic groups were educated together in Polish: not only the Poles, but also the Belarusians, who spoke little or no Polish, and the Jewish children who did. But there was animosity and division between the racial groups in the school playground. 'It was just normal stuff,' Dad says, shrugging off my questions. 'It was like children always do. We didn't know what it was about.' He recalls the Belarusian boys who invited him to play after school and then ambushed him, throwing stones and chasing him as he scampered home across the fields. He remembers also a brief incident with a Jewish girl, beautiful with big brown eyes, who approached him in the playground but then ran away in horror when he shot at her with a homemade toy gun. 'I was so embarrassed, I couldn't think what else to do. The other boys were watching.' Then he pauses, wondering what became of her under the later German occupation. 'Poor thing, maybe she finished up badly. That was a terrible thing for me to do.'

This playground behaviour, sinister or not, reflected the realities beyond the school gate. In the Wiśniewski family's very modest railway house, on the outskirts of Wołynka, my father remembers living 'normally, without animosity' alongside the Jewish community. His Polish parents looked up to their wealthy Jewish neighbours, he believes, and modelled their family ethos—education and hard work as a key to betterment—on the Jewish example. 'Do you know my parents had almost finished building a new house for us in Brześć when the war started?' he says. 'We never got to move in.' But he remembers some Poles who behaved differently, and a number of violent anti-Jewish demonstrations, one in particular in which angry Poles smashed Jewish shop windows after a Jewish butcher stabbed a local policeman. The rumour was—'and who knows whether it was true or not'—the butcher had been caught selling unlicensed meat. Some of this anger my father puts down to the work of activists, people he believes wanted to further destabilise the Kresy's emerging and shaky regional identity. These growing racial tensions were to prove critical in coming years, the region's multi-cultural image a fragile charade.

~

The intensity of Stefania's educational ambition for her children was matched only by her devotion to her faith. The family regularly walked to the church in Brześć for Mass, an hour each way. Roman Catholicism was inescapable and unquestionable, as much a part of the family's life as its Polishness. The happy household events recalled by my father all centred on the religious calendar—Easter and Christmas in particular. Each Christmas Eve, Józef and Stefania's bed was pushed to the side of their one living space and a table large enough to seat the entire family was draped in white linen. Handfuls of hay were pushed under the cloth to symbolise the manger. The family cut and decorated a pine tree with flickering candles and angels, and they would gather and eat together as dusk came on. The 12 courses of the Christmas Eve vigil, Wigilia, were all meat-free: clear beetroot soup (*barszcz*), fish, and egg pasta dumplings called *pierogi* (filled with sauerkraut, potatoes or mushrooms), followed by sweets and cake. Then the family would walk, snow underfoot, stars overhead, the happy distance to midnight Mass. There were no presents, Dad says, 'but we didn't mind. Sometimes we had a lolly.'

Alongside Stefania's faith, though, travelled a superstitious curiosity. Gypsies would occasionally knock at the door of the Wiśniewski cottage selling trinkets and looking for food. His mother would let them in and feed the visitors, even though there was little to spare in their hungry household. Once, he says, Stefania agreed to have her fortune told by a gypsy woman and she sent the children outside to wait while it was done. When the gypsy left, the children were eager to know what their mother had been told.

'I don't know why, but she just wouldn't tell us,' Dad says. 'It couldn't have been good. She was crying.'

My father's siblings—those old enough to remember, those still alive to tell—have their own stories of the petty childhood rivalries and triumphs of those years. Czesiek, older by two years, tells me Stefan was their mother's favourite, a sickly and needy baby who grew into an annoying little brother. Dad, in turn, remembers his two playmates the best, the boys closest to him in age: Czesiek, 'sly, playing up to Mum' for preferential treatment at dinnertime; and Romek, his hero brother, 'into everything, every adventure, but not schoolwork'. Kazik, meanwhile, was too young to take part in his older siblings' rough-and-tumble so he followed his father Józef everywhere. 'If we wanted to find Kazik, we just had to look for my father,' Dad says. 'He worshipped him.' (It seems the adoration was mutual: 'My darling Kazio', my grandfather would address all his letters to his youngest son, almost 30 years later.)

Of Hela's early years, though, little is known. My father remembers his older sister only as lively and vivacious, a teenage 'handful' who had been living away from home for a year before the war with a childless and wealthy aunt, a 'countess' married to another of Józef's brothers. The aunt had offered to adopt Hela; Hela's parents had politely declined. She had arrived back at the little Brześć house impossibly sophisticated, almost unrecognisable to her siblings. Her Polish had lost its rural twang, Dad says, and she knew how to lay a table. Beyond that, he can't elaborate. He cannot retrieve her face from the shadows of the busy room they all shared.

~

Hela was my godmother and my father's favourite sister. But if I ask him what it was about her that was special—what made her stand out from the family crowd of 11 siblings—he is vague and a little uneasy. He doesn't know really, she was just a good person. She was beautiful when she was younger, he adds, as if this is something I need to know.

As a child, it never occurred to me that my aunt and I shared the same name. My own name was so unique and strange, so *me*, that the idea another person might also have grown up with it was implausible. I knew my aunt as everyone else did, by the Polish diminutive, Hela. Perhaps this was just as well. Helena Wiśniewska was a lumpy mouthful in English, not only because of the complex and obviously difficult surname, with its deep, throaty consonants and hidden v's and sh's. Our shared Christian name also offered numerous options for Kiwi mispronunciation. Was it Hel-en-*a*, Hel-*ee*-na or Hel-*ay*-na? To my New Zealand ear, all of these were normal, probably acceptable, if a little awkward. To my aunt, who must have yearned for the effortless flow of Hel-*en*-a, with its French-like emphasis on the soft second vowel, the constant mispronunciation of her Christian name must have been intolerable. Hela, just Hela. Not as beautiful, but less likely to be mangled.

I'm only guessing, of course, what she might have thought. She's been dead many years.

When I grew up, there was little about Ciocia Hela, Aunty Hela, that interested me. She made occasional appearances at family events when I was smaller and then, as I grew up, she almost disappeared from view. I look at photographs of her now and agree that she was—could have been—beautiful. She had the Slavic bone structure all my father's sisters were blessed with, bright blue eyes, soft brown hair. But from my earliest memories, Hela was plain. She wore dowdy clothes, cardigans and crochet hats at a time when no one else did. I don't remember her wearing lipstick like the other women I knew—in fact, she wore no makeup at all. She looked older than she was, more tired than she should have been, and she didn't seem to care. Maybe, I reasoned, this was because she was deeply religious, attending Mass so often—*every day*, my cousins whispered— that it horrified me, despite my own Roman Catholic upbringing. There were crucifixes nailed throughout her house.

Ciocia Hela spoke only a little English. 'How is school?' she would ask me, and then stare blankly as I burbled a response. She didn't understand my chatter. Even if we could have spoken easily there was little to discuss, no intersection in our worlds. She had no children and lived in a small, weatherboard house on a quarter-acre section in Papatoetoe. From the street it wasn't an unusual house—grass lawn at the front, vegetable garden at the rear, white venetian blinds in the windows. Standard roses lined the driveway and a concrete porch led to a glass-panelled front door that few people used. Visitors, like us, always came in the back door by the garage. But inside, the house seemed unnaturally quiet and cold to me. Hela was married to Henek Torbus, an older, ex-Polish army officer, a short, bald man who (it was openly discussed) drank too much. Uncle Henek's English was worse than Hela's, and his awkward interactions with the children who occasionally visited their house were the source of much amusement and mimicry among my cousins, my sister and me.

'Heloooo Helenka,' Uncle Henek bellowed every time I entered their too-tidy living room, pushing himself out of the blue armchair in the corner under the window. I'd stop and await further communication, aware that it would be rude to ignore him and flee, but unwilling to get too close nonetheless. We would eye each other for a moment and then, when his square hand tapped me roughly on the head to signal that our standoff was at an end, I'd run to join my cousins and sister, casting an apologetic smile over my shoulder.

Occasionally, Dad insisted that we stay with my aunt on our family trips to Auckland. On these visits I learned that Hela was a meticulous seamstress who embroidered ornate tablecloths and doilies. Pieces of unfinished work, their shiny threads wound in garish but tidy bundles, were kept in boxes in her sunroom and cupboards throughout the house. Her house smelt of Palmolive soap and the sheets on my bed were uncomfortable starched linen. An ornate marble clock on her living room mantelpiece chimed a spooky song every hour, on the hour, all night. I also learned that Henek and Hela did not share a bed. Even as a child, I realised this meant there were problems with the marriage, problems I couldn't technically explain but which perhaps accounted for the frosty atmosphere in their house. Quietly, I sympathised. Henek had no hair and smelt of whisky. I wasn't surprised Hela wanted a bed of her own; I would too.

I learned also, as I grew older, that she was unwell. Not physically unwell—although maybe there were ailments—but mentally, shamefully, unwell. I didn't know what was wrong. The adults talked about her in hushed voices and there were long periods when I wouldn't see her at all.

Soon after I was married, a few months before my daughter Anna was born, Hela was diagnosed with a brain tumour and died, my distraught father at her bedside. The scale of his distress surprised me. I didn't go to the funeral.

For many years, this was all I knew of the aunt after whom I was named. Of course there were stories about her wartime exile, the same stories of loss, hardship and maybe even bravery that she shared with my father and his siblings. But while my father, at least as far as I could see, was putting that sadness behind him, making an adult life for himself in New Zealand, Hela had always seemed to be on a very different path. What was it that set her on that course? What was it about her that shamed me then and intrigues me now? What might be learned from walking through history again with them as my guides—my elderly father on one arm, my ghostly aunt on the other?

2

By a great, swift water
On a stony bank
A human skull was lying
And shouting: Allah la ilah.

And in that cry such horror
And such supplication
So great was its despair
That I asked the helmsman:

For what can it still cry out? Of what is it still afraid?
What divine judgement could strike it yet again?

Aleksander Wat, 'From Persian Parables'

The quiet city of Brest, Belarus, my father's hometown, is not a city for tourists. I had guessed as much in 1988 when I'd tried to picture it from a riverbank in eastern Poland, and I confirmed it more than 20 years later, in 2009, when I finally visited with my father and my sister, Zofia.

We arrived at midnight in October. Brest's mock-Gothic railway station, with its harsh lighting and prefabricated outbuildings, was too Cold War to be real; it felt like a bizarre film set. Adding to the theatre were the border officials who greeted the tired occupants of our train from Warsaw. They stood behind a flimsy trestle table, overdressed and flamboyant in their blue uniforms and too-big caps, examining our Belarusian visas as if they had never seen them before. Our passports were shuffled between them while they glanced at us, then back at our photos. I had already explained our interest in Brest in our visa applications—we wanted to visit my father's hometown, I'd written—but I didn't know whether we would be expected to answer further questions here. I had nothing to be nervous about, but I was. A queue of impatient locals muttered behind us until the guards finally lost interest in our documents and waved us on.

In the station's silent main hall, under its cathedral-like vaulted ceiling, several people slept huddled under blankets on wooden benches lining the walls. The car park outside was deserted. There were no waiting taxis, no information counters for helpless tourists like us. Out of the gloom, a man in a cap approached, holding a sign with my name on it. In my head I thanked our clever travel agent in Wellington for her foresight as we followed the driver to the car, its make and age unidentifiable in the darkness. The driver wasn't interested in conversation, despite my father's efforts to engage him, and the ride to the hotel was short and silent. At our hotel, a woman at reception with red lipstick and matching hair was similarly terse. She rummaged in the darkness to give us keys attached to wooden tags and pointed, without comment, to the lift on the other side of the hotel's smoky foyer. Men in dark jackets leaned on walls and chatted, eyeing us as we shuffled past with our bags.

'Who do you think they are?' I asked Zofia. 'What are they looking at?'

'They're probably just from the casino next door,' my sister said as the lift doors clanked shut. 'Don't worry about it.'

I'd always known Zofia would be more open to Brest's charms than I would. Maybe she hadn't read my guidebook as thoroughly as I had. The country's KGB atmosphere, the book said, was its chief tourist attraction. Belarus was a 'hermetically sealed Soviet time capsule' run by the same dictator, Alexander

Lukashenko, for 15 years. It was one of the last places in the world where travellers could get a taste of old-school communism. To me, this was a poor recommendation, but to Zofia it was a challenge.

'Come on, this will be interesting,' she said, when I grimaced at the mould in the bathroom of our sixth-floor room, the green rotary telephone and its thick curly cord. 'Toughen up.'

This wasn't the first hotel room my sister and I had shared on that trip. We'd been tiptoeing around each other's bags and beds for 12 days, revisiting some of the Polish sights I'd seen on previous trips, uncomfortably aware of the years that had passed since we last slept side by side. We'd forgotten what it was like to travel without our husbands and children, and forgotten how to be together. Each night, Zofia squeezed earplugs into her ears before climbing into bed and I'd listened to her slow, steady breathing for hours in the dark, wondering how she managed to sleep so soundly, so emphatically. She woke early and would be dressed and tidying her suitcase by the time I began to rouse each morning. As children we had shared rooms, clothes, back seats and ice creams in a muddle of screams, snarls and laughter. We were blond and dark, older and younger, but everything fitted easily. Now, as adults, we were more tolerant of one another but also more aware of our differences.

In Poland, Zofia had paid little attention to relatives who warned us to take care in Belarus. Our cousin Wojtek, who had once again hosted us for part of our journey, had lived most of his life in Soviet-controlled communist Poland and had no desire to reacquaint himself with its bleakness, regardless of family history. He had never been to Belarus; it was 'much too Soviet-style', he said. But we should make sure we carried our passports with us all the time and leave some bags behind in Poland. 'They'll just get stolen if you leave them in a Belarus hotel room,' Wojtek warned.

But my sister was nonplussed. We were only going for two days, she said, what could really go wrong?

'It will be a little adventure,' she assured me.

~

It's nothing new, Zofia's quiet determination, but it took me years to recognise it and to realise that I lacked it. I remember when I saw it in her for the first time.

In 1981, when she was just 17, my sister arrived in Wellington ready to start a law degree. I was 18, an arts student and already a veteran of the city. I'd left Whakatane in a messy flurry the year before. Just before final school exams, I'd been turned down for a journalism course in Wellington and had spent many hours in my room, face pressed to my pillow. It was the first time I had failed at anything and I had no idea what to do with my life. I could hear my parents through the uninsulated walls to the kitchen, losing patience with the melodrama.

'Why doesn't she just go to university?' my father was saying, while my mother put dishes in cupboards. 'She's got a room in a hostel, she could do a real degree.'

'Let her work that one out,' my mother said. 'She'll come around.'

A year later, by the time my sister arrived in Wellington, I was beginning to realise that city and university life suited me. Wellington had what my hometown lacked: a seediness that didn't seem accidental. It was interesting and people liked it that way. No one knew me, or my family, but for the first time my peers seemed intrigued by my unpronounceable surname. It was a point of difference, no longer a burden, and it marked me out from the crowd. My fellow students were interesting too. One thing I'd learned in a year as an undergraduate was that there was a definite hierarchy. Law students—the successful ones at least—were savvy people, worldly and focused. Lots of them had been to private schools. They worked harder; they dressed more smartly. My little sister, who had been the less academic of the two of us at school, didn't seem a likely candidate. The beach-and-beer teenage life of Whakatane had always suited her more than me. She never seemed to get bored sitting on bonnets in beachside car parks with friends, with Meat Loaf's 'Bat Out of Hell' booming from cassette stereos. Zofia was a good sort who gave things a go. Boys in my class would ask me to parties if my sister came. It was me, not Zofia, who couldn't wait to leave.

So if I hadn't thought about studying law, why had she? Where did the idea come from? It certainly wasn't from our parents. The only lawyer we had known was the quiet husband of my mother's librarian friend, Jean. Zofia had spent the summer before university filing documents for Peter in his high-windowed rooms on one of Whakatane's commercial side streets. Maybe this real-life legal experience had been more inspiring than it sounded? It wasn't. Years later she told me her career choice was sparked by a TV show, the glamorous 1970s legal drama *Paperchase*. 'It was a great show,' she told me, 'and I liked their clothes. I didn't know the first thing about law.' In any case, I was as impressed by her gutsy choice of degree as I was surprised by her decision to join me in Wellington. I was even more impressed when she failed a key paper in her first year and decided to repeat it the year after. She was braver than I was; I would never have risked another failure. When she passed, she didn't look back. She went on to graduate with a double degree in 1987.

I finished my less demanding degree before she did and eventually found my way into a postgraduate journalism course and a job. By the time Zofia had finished her studies I was working in London and living with James, and I'd already made my first trip to Poland with Dad. When I returned to Wellington in 1989, Zofia and I spent only three months in the same country before she left for London. She came back to be bridesmaid at my wedding in 1991, and then returned to New Zealand for good in 1995. My daughter Anna, aged five, was flower girl when Zofia and Charlie married at the same wooden Wellington church I had six years earlier. Now, my sister is a senior solicitor at Inland Revenue with a Master's degree in tax law. And here we both are, the middle-aged wives of sensible Kiwi men, with six children between us. We are still fussing about on the fringes of our parents' lives, worrying about our own.

I'm aware, though, that my sister doesn't share my preoccupation with tracing the loops and circles in our family history. It's not that she isn't interested; she has as much at stake in the past as I do. She was with me when we climbed off that train in Belarus, and I know she would have come on other journeys if she'd been able. But Zofia is busy, with a hefty mortgage to pay, and has less time for research and speculation. She has had to plot her career as carefully as the weekly dinner menus that appear under a magnet on her family fridge every Sunday night. I, on the other hand, have drifted through jobs, steadily reducing the hours and intensity of work as my children have grown. This space to think, I know, is a luxury.

'How's it going? All the research?' Zofia will ask me.

'Slowly. It's complicated.'

Somewhere along the line, my sister went as far as she could. My father and I, on the other hand, are still heading eastwards. There may not even be a destination. Maybe there will just be a journey.

~

The following morning's weak autumn sunshine confirmed my dismal first impressions of Brest. The Hotel Intourist was even less attractive in daylight, a blank block of socialist realist architecture on a wide thoroughfare, a broken fountain in its car park. Life-sized bronze children danced around an empty pool littered with autumn leaves. The three of us stood on the street wondering where to go first. In each direction, tidy streets were lined with blank-windowed buildings and badly lit stores. Locals wearing stilettos and leather jackets brushed past us, averting their eyes when they heard us speaking English. It was as if they were unaware their city was only a few kilometres away from modern Europe. To the west, and across the broad, slow-moving Bug River skirting the city, was Poland, its back firmly turned on its poorer eastern neighbour.

My father tapped on the driver's window of a taxi parked outside our hotel.

'Can you take us to Wołynka?' he called through the glass. 'Wołynka?'

The driver, his face too young for his handlebar moustache, folded his newspaper and gestured to my father to take the seat next to him. He was happy to take the fare and wasn't going to ask why this trio of foreigners—an old man and his two middle-aged daughters—would want to go to the village on the other side of the river. Dad didn't wait for his questions, but began an explanation in Russian as soon as he took his seat. I assumed he was telling the driver the story he had tried to tell everyone we had met so far: he was looking for the site of his old family home from before the war. The driver nodded as he listened, but remained mute as we pulled out of the hotel car park.

I had developed a new respect for my father's linguistic abilities on that trip. I'd already known our relatives were impressed with his beautiful, old-fashioned Polish, but now, for the first time, I'd heard him conversing fluently in Russian. When had he learned to speak a third language? And how, I wondered, had my father turned 79 without me ever realising he could? I had to admit, I was impressed. I'd struggled with French as a teenager, thankfully giving it up when it became clear I had no aptitude for it. I still couldn't speak Polish. I wondered now, though, what father I would have known if my first language had been the same as his. Was he a different man when he spoke the language of his childhood? It seemed sometimes he was; here, in Belarus, he certainly wasn't the father I thought I knew.

The taxi took us through the orderly streets of Brest and across the bridge that spanned the broad Mukhavyets River, a tributary of the Bug. We followed signs leading to the Belarusian–Polish border, but at the roundabout near the border post we turned away from the main highway to follow a smaller road leading south through the flat fields. Our first view of Wołynka from the taxi window was of a collection of mismatched wooden cottages lining the narrow road. The older, traditional buildings with their dark timber exteriors looked empty, their gardens overgrown. The few newer homes, many half built, also seemed abandoned. On one corner a grocery store looked shut, on another the domed spire of a Russian Orthodox church loomed over its low-rise neighbours. This used to be a Jewish town, my father said, where the shops were. 'Very busy, nice houses,' he told us, quietly, while I took in the desolation outside. There were no people anywhere. The Jewish shop owners, like their Polish customers, no longer existed in Wołynka. Despite the late autumn sunshine, I felt chilled.

'Stop! It's here! Stop here!' My father's loud voice startled the driver, who pulled to the side of the road, puzzled by instructions that were suddenly coming in English.

'No—not here! A bit further down, by that tree!'

The car pulled over a second time, near a dirt lane that led away from the sealed road. In front of us and across the low fields I could see the skyline of Brest. Behind us were the fringes of the village of Wołynka, more little houses, and scrubby gardens.

My father was already out of the car, pacing through the long grass on the side of the road. 'This is it,' he said. 'We've found it.' Zofia and I followed him onto the grass, and even the taxi driver climbed out of the car to watch.

'This is where the house was, just here.' My father gestured at a grassy mound just below the road. He climbed it and searched the horizon, as if on a viewing platform, looking for familiar landmarks. 'These were our fields, this was where we played.'

There was nothing to see but grass and a tree, still green-leafed.

'I think this was our tree, our pear tree,' Dad said, and then: 'Actually, I'm not sure.' He was muttering, walking in circles. I was worried. Did he really know where we were? The road stretched several kilometres into the distance, the landscape flat and unchanging in both directions. The spot could easily have been another 100 metres that way—or that. There was no sign of a house having been there. How did he know it was here? Because of the railway line, he said. They lived in a railway house. He took me by the arm to the road and there, still visible within the tarseal, were two steel tracks. They made a diagonal scar across its width and then ended abruptly at the grass verge. The trains, like the man who once raised and lowered the barrier arm for local traffic, were gone.

Even this proof didn't shake my disappointment. I couldn't reconcile what I had imagined—a place built in my mind over many years, picture by picture, through my father's stories—with what I was now seeing. I'd always known the country idyll he'd described to me no longer existed. The little house, the chickens and squealing, happy children were shadows and ghosts. But the reality of its absence left me feeling cheated. I had come so far, for this. Soviet apartment blocks on the horizon were dark, lumpy blurs in the background of our photographs. Scraps of litter lay curling in the grass. The village—the empty field—was as unwelcoming as the city on the skyline. My family's past in this place was not only gone, I thought, it was as if it had never been.

If Dad sensed how I was feeling, he didn't show it. He couldn't hide his pleasure at being there. Zofia and I watched him pace about and take more photos; I took some of him, the taxi driver took one of the three of us. As I followed his tracks through the bent grass, I kicked what appeared to be a small piece of red brick and concrete; maybe it was a bit of the old house chimney or its foundations. When I picked it up, my father seemed momentarily interested. Then he waved it away. It was such a long time ago, he said, almost 70 years. But on the short drive back to Brest I slipped the piece of brick into my pocket.

It wasn't until later that evening, in the weak light of my hotel room, that I realised my souvenir was no longer in my coat pocket. I remembered feeling its roughness between my fingers as we walked along the city's broad boulevards that afternoon. I wondered where I had dropped it. Perhaps I would be able to retrace our steps tomorrow, even go back to the site of the old house and collect another. I knew my father would be happy to do that. But the idea of a return visit depressed me. I had finished with Wołynka, I decided, just as Wołynka seemed to have finished with me. I wouldn't mention the missing souvenir to anyone.

Then I pulled the stiff, cheap hotel curtains on the darkening sky outside and caught a final glimpse of the shining highway beneath us, the long road to Minsk. It stretched east like a glittering trail as far as the horizon.

~

Eastern Poland, 1988, on a road trip break: Kazik, Jasia, Wacek and Helena.

Zofia, Stefan and Helena pose for the taxi driver at the site of the old
Wiśniewski house near Brest, Belarus, 2009.
Soviet apartment blocks were dark, lumpy blurs in the background.

Brest's historic fortress was the only must-see attraction listed in our city guidebook, and one of the few remaining landmarks in the city that my father remembered. When the taxi driver left us near the fortress entrance the next day, the car park was cold and empty of vehicles, the sky a threatening grey.

There was almost nothing left of the fortifications that once surrounded the 19th-century site. Instead, we entered through a much more recent construction, a tunnel in the shape of the red star, the symbol of the Soviet military. It was an eerily impressive if contrived entry, the dark space inside livened by a recorded soundtrack of gunfire and the violent screams of battle. In the late afternoon light inside the fortress, we walked silently past old Soviet tanks and guns lining each side of a wide walkway, our hands occasionally reaching out to brush their cold metal as we passed. At the end of the walkway, the memorial to the fortress's World War II Soviet heroes towered over us, impossible to miss: a monstrous soldier's face frozen in open-mouthed angst, one of the largest Soviet monuments ever erected. Russian orchestral marches blared from loud speakers, the sound fading to a tinny beat as we walked on. Inside a section of the former barracks, the last of the fortress's few remaining buildings, Dad groaned when I asked him to translate a Russian sign bolted to the wall above a low door.

'I don't know what it says,' he said. 'Stop asking me.'

He could speak Russian, he said, but he'd forgotten how to read its Cyrillic script. And this Soviet rebranding of a childhood landmark was new and unwelcome. He remembered a 'citadel', with castle-like red brick walls and trees, not a sprawling ruin.

Outside the barracks I stopped to watch a local bride posing alone for photographs. Below the broken red brick walls, the stark white tulle of her dress brushed on the dead grass and I wondered again why my grandparents had chosen to raise their family here. It must have been—despite the confidence of the new Polish authorities—an area notorious for its instability, even by Polish standards. Brześć had a long and turbulent history of bloodshed and the very existence of the fortress was evidence that it had been at the heart of much of that destruction. Even when my father was a child, when the fortress still housed Polish army officers and a storage depot, it was scarred and damaged from its World War I wounds. In 1939, the last of the Polish army defenders had held their ground for three days inside its walls against the German invaders. Then, in the summer of 1941, it was the site of the doomed defence by 800 Soviet soldiers against the German Wehrmacht. The citadel, once safely back in Russian hands after the war, had been renamed Hero Fortress to commemorate that World War II Soviet tragedy. But its earlier and equally gruesome history, like my father's life here, had now been forgotten.

It was getting colder and a light drizzle was falling as we left. In the car park, noisy Belarusian schoolchildren waited behind the steamy windows of a bus, anticipating fresh air and freedom. While we walked, my father told me about visiting the citadel as a schoolchild himself before the war, part of an organised summertime camp.

'They let us play outside the walls, in the forest,' he said. 'We played chasing games, things like that.' He stopped walking for a moment, to take a breath, as if he was trying to recall the Polish equivalent of cowboys and Indians, or cops and robbers. 'Anyway, when we were running around we found skulls under the leaves in the forest. Big white skulls, five or six of them,' he said.

'Skulls? Human skulls?'

'Well, I suppose they must have been,' he said. 'I don't know what other kind of skulls they could be. We didn't think much about it.'

'What did you do?'

'Nothing. We played with them. We kicked them, like soccer balls.'

'But that's awful.' I was trying to find the right words to respond to this new story, failing. I pictured a group of little boys giggling and shrieking in that once Polish, now Belarusian forest, kicking at the chalky bones, playing their macabre game of football. Whose remains were they? What horror led to their careless disposal? Why would my father react so insensitively to such a grisly discovery?

Dad didn't know the answer to these questions. He was upset that I was so revolted. 'I told you, we didn't think about it, it's just what it was,' he said, avoiding my eyes. 'It's just the way it was.'

Then he was kicking at skulls, and not talking to me any more.

~

The warning signs may have been there, in the gypsy forecasts or the fortress skulls, but they went unheeded: life didn't change for my father until September 1939. He was 10 years old. This is how he thinks of it: the start of the war was the end of his childhood. The family knew that war was imminent, he says, though there was no radio in the house or regular access to newspapers. Word had got to them through the grapevine. He remembers his mother sobbing at the news and his surprise at her tearful reaction. Didn't she know that Poland would win?

Stefan's two older brothers, Florian and Benek, were the first to leave the household, conscripted to the Polish army shortly after the German invasion on 1 September. Within weeks the fighting reached Poland's eastern borders. The family was forced to clear the debris from old World War I concrete bunkers in the fields behind the house, taking shelter there while the worst of the shelling and artillery fire whistled overhead. All the while, Polish civilians from the west and army personnel streamed past the Wiśniewski door, heading east, fleeing the German invasion.

Stefan took up a post outside the house when he could, watching this human flood with curiosity, even excitement. Was he frightened? 'No, not really,' he says, and then more emphatically, 'No, not at all. Something was happening.' When one of those passers-by, a uniformed Polish officer, asked him to run a message to a building near the city, the request was eagerly accepted. Stefan sprinted across the flat and familiar fields towards Brześć, the unread and top-secret message in his pocket. He dropped it safely into an unnamed hand in the building he'd been sent to, and began the sprint home. But he was caught short. German planes attacked the road near the fields, dropping cluster bombs and shooting at civilian refugees and soldiers indiscriminately. My young father hid in a creek until it was over. He was just lucky, he realises now, as the creek would have offered no protection against the German fire. But when he emerged, unscathed, he was shocked by the blood and carnage around him: refugees, soldiers, trucks and horses— 'even horses'—were 'all blown to pieces'. He had completed his mysterious patriotic mission, but this was what real war looked like. Terrified now, he ran home.

The Polish army held out against the German attack on Brześć for three days. Just as it was about to surrender to the superior German forces, word came that the Red Army was advancing from the east. The Soviet Union, in an action agreed with Germany, was invading the Kresy to 'defend' the region's Ukrainians and Belarusians from the Poles. On the evening of 17 September, German and Russian forces staged a joint victory march down the city's broad streets. The following day, the German invaders left, heading westwards, and an eerie calm was left in their wake. It was a short-lived break in the chaos. My father remembers the mass arrival a few days later of the underwhelming Russian conquerors. After the smart and well-equipped German invaders, the Russian soldiers were disappointing. 'They looked terrible,' my father says, 'so awful.' Old rifles were held to their chests with pieces of string rather than leather straps; many had no boots. Some were starving and begged locals for food. 'They couldn't get over how well off we were,' Dad says, laughing now. 'Us!'

The German invaders had made few demands of the Poles during their short stay, but the Russian forces, despite appearances, were not as easily accommodated. The aim was to impose a revolution from abroad, to transform all of the Kresy's previous political, economic and social structures. At first, the Ukrainians and Belarusians welcomed the end of Polish rule, but it became clear that their independence was not part of the Soviet plan. Within months, Soviet citizenship was announced for the entire population of the region. Changes happened rapidly. All symbols of the Polish state—memorials, signs and institutions—were removed and replaced by their Soviet equivalents. Property was confiscated, food supplies dwindled, and all use of the Polish language was forbidden. 'Re-education' was a critical part of the plan. Dad remembers that school continued but the syllabus was transformed. Classes centred on Russian propaganda, and he was angered and unconvinced by the long, dull and pointless lessons. It was during this time that he reluctantly developed his Russian language skills. A catchy Russian song he taught to my sister and me as children, one we would sing noisily and happily in the back seat of the family car, celebrated the glories of the strong and vigorous fir trees grown in Soviet collective forests. (I had always thought we were singing a Polish song, I tell him now, something about a Christmas tree. 'But it's Russian,' he says. 'Can't you tell?')

The miseries of life under Soviet rule were many, but it was clear the alternatives to occupation were worse. There were no complaints about the new regime, not even at home. 'Nobody was able to speak their mind,' Dad says, 'because everyone was watching everyone else, and who knows what a child might repeat. Things were very uncertain. They were taking people away.' The new authorities believed large numbers of Polish nationals in the Kresy were unreservedly hostile to Soviet socialist ideology: policemen, teachers, doctors and local government officials were being taken from their homes. The families of these enemies of the Soviet state, their wives and children, were among the first wave of mass civilian deportees to Siberia who left Brześć railway station in the depths of the winter of 1940. As the civilian deportations continued over that year, in what seemed to be deliberately planned waves of night-time disappearances, the fear among locals increased: no one was sure of the criteria for selection. In the stress and uncertainty of this new socialist world, old racial animosities became openly aired. My father remembers the Poles' growing mistrust of their Jewish neighbours. The Jewish Poles believed they were 'much better off' under Soviet rather than Nazi occupation and many were cooperating with the occupying Soviet forces, Dad says. He is unequivocal about this 'treachery'. Some Jews—even boys who used to go to school with his older brothers—wore the red armbands that signified their NKVD, or Russian secret police, association. And many Jews held grudges against the Poles who hadn't, he concedes, treated them well before the war.

'Maybe the Jews didn't like what the Poles had been doing to them,' he says. 'I don't know.'

After almost 18 months of Russian occupation, Józef and Stefania were cautiously optimistic. Perhaps they'd been spared the worst; they were still in Poland, still alive. There had been no word from their two older sons, but the family was otherwise intact. Life was increasingly difficult, but bearable. Perhaps the

Russian authorities felt the railway man and his family posed little threat to the socialist dream. On a summer evening in June 1941, the evening that was to be their last in the little house, my father would have gone to sleep praying for Poland's safe delivery from the loathed Russian invaders. His mother, I think, would have been giving thanks that they were still together, at home.

This is the story as my father tells it, the way he remembers it. The books I read on the Poles' experience of the war in this region support his memories. The Luftwaffe did shoot at civilians as well as the Polish armed forces in the chaos of the German invasion. The flight of civilians eastwards did clog up roads and hamper the Polish retreat. I ask him questions and he gives me answers, but—again—he can't be drawn on detail. What did the Polish army officer who gave him the secret message look like? He doesn't remember; it was too long ago. Where was the building he was sent to? Just a building in town; why do I need to know this? How did he feel, a ten-year-old boy, witnessing death for the first time? Terrible, of course, he says. But much worse was to come, much worse.

And then, hovering between us, are the unasked questions. Historians agree that Polish anti-Semitism was ugly in the Kresy during the period of my father's childhood. Many argue that the Jewish distrust and dislike of the Poles was mutual. But I find myself unwilling to ask Dad to elaborate on the resentment he and his family felt towards their richer Jewish neighbours. I listen without comment to his stories of Jewish collusion with the Soviet occupiers. What am I afraid of? Maybe I'm afraid I'll hear something I wish I hadn't. Maybe I'll hear the voice of the boy who saw his mother buying supplies from Jewish merchants with smarter houses and prettier daughters. Maybe he will tell me again that the Poles were to suffer as much as the Jews did. Maybe I'm afraid I will believe him.

3

The porch whose doors face the west
Has large windows. The sun warms it well.

Czesław Miłosz, 'The Porch'

My daughter Anna, now 21 years old, says she remembers the moment she grew up. It was when she realised—in a 'flash like a light going on'—that her father and I had been alive before her, that our world didn't start when hers did and that her parents had already had friends, little sisters, scraped knees, hangovers and essays of our own before her. She's embarrassed when she tells me this, tucking her hair behind her ear, smiling, leaning back on the kitchen counter, and wondering if this admission makes her seem silly.

I tell her I know what she means. Growing up is all about separating from your parents, working out you are your own person, I say.

What I also want to say, but don't, is that it doesn't mean you stop wondering about before. After all, *before* might hold answers to the questions you never knew you wanted to ask.

Being Polish in Brześć in 1941 was a misfortune for my father, but being Polish in small-town New Zealand 20 years later had its own challenges. It was a puzzling affliction, drawing some sympathy but little curiosity.

Dad had ended up in Whakatane, my pretty but end-of-the-road hometown, in much the same way he'd arrived at all places: washed in on a tide of coincidence and convenience. He'd been offered work in the late 1950s, first at Kinleith in nearby Kawerau, and then at Whakatane's pulp and paper mill on the river. The money in Whakatane was tempting, a flat was on offer and the timing was good. He had just met and was about to marry my mother, Olga.

Olga Zam, an Aucklander, was the New Zealand-born daughter of another European immigrant, a Jewish tailor from Russia. She and my father met at a party thrown by his Polish friends. Maybe it was Olga's familiar European features that first attracted Stefan: he doesn't deny it when I suggest it. She was beautiful, he says, with her deep brown eyes and high cheekbones. In photos from that time, my mother is almost unrecognisable: elegant in shimmering sleeveless evening dresses, a cigarette dipping at a stylish angle between her fingers, her lips a deep red. For my father at least, it was love at first sight. He drove her home from the party and they were married six months later.

My mother was drawn to my father for similar reasons. She understood his voice, his Eastern European temperament. This olive-skinned, blue-eyed man with foreign features reminded her of her own father. Stefan was serious and had ambitions that the Kiwi boys she knew didn't have. She liked his accent. But Olga, like her new fiancé, had a tragic childhood of her own. She, too, was looking for a fresh start. The relationship between my parents, both damaged people, was destined to be rocky.

~

I haven't the heart now to tell my father that my earliest memories of him are fearful. In those recollections I'm with him, not my mother, at events involving screeching engines and people with blank faces. Sometimes we're at air shows, where monstrous black shadows squeal and loop overhead; sometimes we're at beachside races, where powerboats threaten to lift out of the water and flip towards us in slow-motion somersaults. But almost as vivid as my memory of fear is the sense of my father as shelter: the arms that lifted me, the warm neck I buried my face in.

As I grew, though, he couldn't protect me from the terror of things I had yet to encounter. I couldn't see them but I knew they were there, in the dark outside my bedroom window: tsunamis, hell, a future without parents. The fear began when my father knelt by my bed at night, patiently and insistently teaching my little sister and me to recite the Lord's Prayer, line by line, in a language that made no sense and was comically impossible to mouth. I was shocked in later years when I saw the Polish text: *Ojcze nasz, któryś jest w niebie, święć się imię Twoje.* Our Father, who art in heaven, hallowed be thy name. The mashed-up words looked nothing like the sounds I'd been making. What was it that my father thought God was needed for? Wasn't everything okay as it was? It began to make more sense when I learned what had happened to him as a child: a terrible adventure, something to do with the war. He told us disjointed stories about soldiers in the night, a train with no windows, hunger. I remember my distaste for these stories and the sense that they were being forced on me. I wasn't interested in their frightening lessons. I wanted to believe everything was all right, all over, and that my father was the hero of a sad fairy tale now living happily ever after in New Zealand.

But Dad's story wouldn't go away. I made silent lists in my head when I went to bed and couldn't sleep: What to Take When the Russians Come. Unlike my father, I'd be prepared. Socks, my warmest coat, my favourite water crackers, pyjamas. Would I need pyjamas in Siberia? The nuns and priests at my little Catholic primary school fed my anxieties. The nuns were supernatural beings whose sallow skin, dark brown robes and wimples were disguises that hid their magical talents. At any moment, I expected one of them to whisk skyward like the wonderful Sally Field, the flying nun who appeared on our black-and-white TV every week. When the priests told us, with serious faces, stories in which good children who said their prayers were lifted to heaven on beams of light or encountered visions of Our Lady in shady grottos, I believed them. All the adults I knew seemed to believe them, my father especially so. Sunday Mass, with its familiar ritual of best clothes, sing-along songs and bacon and eggs afterwards, was no hardship for me. Neither was our nightly prayer ritual. It was an insurance policy against harm, I thought. *Give us this day our daily bread*, my father said, in Polish and in English, and my sister and I obediently chanted after him. I knew, because he told me, that had it not been for God, I would not have been born. My father would not be alive had God not saved him from starvation. I prayed frequently and fervently: I prayed not to get fillings at visits to the dental nurse; I prayed that the Russians would knock on someone else's door. I prayed for my parents to stay married and not die.

~

My mother was born in 1934, the single offspring of her parents, Joseph and Grace Zam. She has no idea what prompted the couple to name their newborn baby girl Olga, and suspects it was her Russian Jewish father, not her New Zealand-born mother, who might have had the final say. But its choice might indicate the balance of power in Joseph and Grace's ill-fated relationship. Before Olga turned five, her mother would be gone.

Joseph was a tailor and Queen Street businessman, a short, slight man, with a heavy Russian accent and a pronounced limp caused by a mysterious childhood accident. He had been born in 1893 in Feodosiya, a Crimean port city with a long Jewish history on the Black Sea in what was then Russia, and now, controversially, the Ukraine. Joseph was one of eight children in the Zam household, a family of businessmen and craftsmen. His father Aaron was a watchmaker, as was his grandfather, Nathan. A photograph of a family picnic in the first years of the new century shows well-dressed people gathered under large trees, reclining in long grass around a glistening silver samovar. To the left of the family group, in a smart suit and carefully tipped hat, is my young grandfather. The family was clearly well to do. But it was a bad time to be Jewish in Russia, wealthy or not. Anti-Jewish violence and looting broke out in Feodosiya in 1905, just one of the many pogroms that took place in Russia over that time. No one knows when the family fled, but by 1915 Aaron and his wife Hannah Zam, along with their oldest son Alexander, a master tailor, were living in Glasgow, Scotland. By 1923, younger son Joseph was living and working in Auckland, also as a tailor, having arrived into Wellington with his sister Lizbeth, or Liza, on the *Rotorua* in 1916.

Mum doesn't remember her father as a particularly Jewish man. His extended family was rarely mentioned and, as far as she knew, he never attended a synagogue or socialised with other members of the Jewish community in Auckland. As a child, she attended a number of different schools and had a mixed and typically Kiwi religious education based on broad Christian principles and occasional Sunday School lessons. At the age of 15, she left school to work for her father, whom she remembers only as a hard worker and a demanding employer. His busy workroom was on the third floor of the Sunday School Union building on Queen Street, close to the town hall, where he produced bespoke and off-the-rack suits for Aucklanders looking for European styling. At its peak, and driven by the

Above: Zam family picnic, Feodosiya, Crimea, circa 1912.

Below: Joseph and Liza.

Right: Joseph Zam, tailor, Scotland, circa 1915.

Below left: Grace Zam, with baby Olga, 1934.

Below right: Olga, aged 4, with Joseph Zam at Marlborough St, Mt Eden, 1939.

surge in demand for suiting after World War II, Joseph's 'Worthy Tailors' employed about 50 full-time staff.

Despite his business success, the limping and balding Joseph would never have been a good match for my much younger and excitable grandmother. Grace Cowley was a headstrong Auckland girl with waves of cocoa-coloured hair and strange but arrestingly mismatched eyes—one blue and one brown. *Heterochromia iridis* sounds unfortunate, but it isn't. Grace's odd eyes were probably the result of a very rare, but harmless, hereditary accident. The few people who knew her say she was a ballroom dancer who liked attention, and she enjoyed her memorable eyes. Perhaps it was her eyes that attracted Joseph; it certainly wasn't her love of dancing. Remembering the limping Joseph, my mother thinks this alone would have doomed the marriage. She has only one shadowy memory of Grace. In it, she's clinging to her glamorous mother's hand while her father, in a fury, throws and smashes dinner plates in the family kitchen. In 1938, when Olga was four years old, Grace left the small family home in Marlborough Street, Mount Eden, and didn't return. She was to have a number of other relationships, including another marriage, before she died in 1978. She also had another daughter in 1944, named much more conventionally than her first: Robyn. Neither my mother nor her half-sister knew of each other's existence, or the extent of their mother's secrets, until many years after Grace's death. Grace's departure from Mum's life at the time was permanent and, even today, unexplained.

In one black-and-white photo given to my mother in recent years by Robyn, Grace is staring boldly at the camera, an older woman with Mum's aging features. One eye is clearly lighter than the other. When I look at this photo, I think the colloquial alternatives for *Heterochromia iridis* are apt: *odd eyes, cat eyes*. Grace was certainly secretive and wild; she fled when she was cornered and hid well when she was threatened. Was it just

66

coincidence, or did her unusual eyes filter the world in a different way, with a feline wariness? Until he died, Joseph refused to discuss Grace with his grieving daughter and stubbornly maintained his silence on her whereabouts or his past life with her.

'He just told me she was dead,' Mum says. 'So I gave up asking.'

After his divorce from Grace, Joseph married another New Zealander, also a divorcee, Isabella Barnett. She was the housekeeper Joseph had hired to live in and manage domestic duties in Grace's absence. Isabella was also the mother of Janice, a fair-skinned and freckled girl with peaky features, almost the same age as my dark-eyed, dark-haired mother. Olga was fond of her new stepsister and the two girls had a good relationship, Mum says. But Joseph couldn't hide his favouritism: Olga was his daughter, Janice wasn't. Isabella, similarly, never cared for Olga and, according to my mother, actively discouraged the girls' friendship. 'She poisoned my relationship with Janice,' Mum says, 'the way she did with anything that might have made me happy.'

It's difficult for me to share my mother's loathing of this stranger. I look at the few photos I can find of Isabella and see only a plain, pinched-looking woman on the fringes of family outings, sitting on picnic rugs with children and food, my young mother nowhere near. Isabella looks as unhappy as her stepdaughter, I think; she is a woman trapped in a miserable marriage. But even as Mum nears 80 years of age herself, she wonders openly how her life might have been had her father never remarried. 'The old woman,' she says with surprising venom every time Isabella is referred to.

During the war, and shortly after Joseph's marriage to Isabella, Olga was offered a home with her father's childless and now wealthy brother, Alexander, or Alec, who lived in Potts

Point, Sydney. Mum believes it would have been an escape from the complications of Joseph's newly blended family and her vindictive stepmother. She has kept a copy of the letter her uncle wrote to his brother, a well-thumbed and yellowed document, more evidence of Isabella's treachery. In it, Alec writes in oddly formal English handwriting to 'Joe', complaining about his brother's lack of a response to a previous letter. A mutual friend had told him all about Joe's little girl, he writes, and 'how clever she is . . . Lizzie and I would like to give her all the education and bring her up as our own child, she would have all the opportunity.' Another friend would be in Auckland in four weeks' time to collect Olga, if Joseph agreed. But Mum remembers her stepmother taking her aside, out of earshot of her father, and terrifying her with stories of snakes and spiders in Australia. 'She told me it was a terrible, dangerous place. She told me I would hate Australia. So when my father asked if I wanted to go to my uncle, I refused, and they never asked again.'

Isabella has been dead many years, but her treatment of my young mother remains unforgiven. I suggest to Mum that Joseph may have been as much to blame; he clearly failed to protect his daughter from his unhappy new wife. But she will not be drawn to criticise her father for this. Joseph had a weakness for gambling, she admits, in particular for the horses. And there was a time when he mysteriously disappeared from the family home when Olga was a teenager, to return six months later subdued and aged amid whispered adult tales of prison time for black-market dealings in imported fabric. When he died, he left only a little money and few possessions for the dysfunctional family to squabble over. 'I think it was the gambling that was his downfall in the end,' Mum says.

Joseph and Isabella had two sons together, Olga's half-brothers, John and Buddy, but it was an unhappy household. When my mother was a teenager, shortly after her father's return from his unexplained absence, Isabella had another baby, Christine. There were deep problems in the marriage at this point: Joseph believed the new baby wasn't his. When tensions in the house became unbearable, Mum left to board with family friends and, shortly afterwards, Joseph's second marriage collapsed. Isabella and her children left the house, and my mother returned home to her father. They were, once again, on their own.

~

In November 1945, on her 21st birthday, Olga received a cheque in the mail for 30 pounds from an insurance company. It was a mysterious and unexplained endowment from her mother, Grace. Olga failed at the time to take advantage of this opportunity to reconnect—a decision she now regrets, more than 30 years after her mother's death. She decided instead to use the money to buy herself a new wool coat in a striking orange colour and with a modern, swing style.

'I didn't tell my father where I got the money to buy it,' Mum says. 'But he hated that coat.'

~

Mum wants me to come with her to Karori Cemetery; she thinks her grandmother is buried there. I tuck the phone under my chin while I finish the breakfast dishes.

'Which grandmother?' I ask.

She sighs. 'My father's mother, of course. Hannah.'

I try to piece it all together: Hannah, Joseph's mother, Aaron's wife. 'I thought she died in Scotland,' I say.

Mum sighs again, upset that I haven't kept up with developments, her piecing together of the Zam family puzzle. 'No, she came to Wellington to live with her daughter Liza, my aunt, when her husband died. She died here,' Mum explains. 'She's in the Jewish cemetery.'

I've only been to one Jewish cemetery before, also with my mother. Shortly after the trip to Belarus with Dad in 2009, in a year that once again favoured explorations of Wiśniewski family history, Zofia and I took Mum to Auckland for a weekend. The aim was to spend some time with her and to visit some of the places from her childhood. It was a walk through a lonely history. In Mt Eden, Mum seemed shocked by the little-changed façade of her old family home. She stood on the footpath opposite, staring at its wooden porch, explaining how she'd had a photograph taken more than 50 years earlier on the same steps. 'You remember that photo, don't you?' she asked Zofia and me. We didn't remember it, we said. We were conscious of time passing and the possibility that the owners of the house, if they were at home, might find our extended scrutiny unnerving. 'I know you've seen it,' Mum continued, exasperated now. 'You must remember it.' At the Sunday School Union Building on Queen Street we climbed the three storeys to her father's old workshop, trying to imagine Joseph with his tape measure and wall mirror in the faded but light-filled atrium of his top floor offices. And then, with a map from Waikumete Cemetery's information desk in our hands, we walked the long lanes of Hebrew graves to Joseph's unmarked plot. This time it was me who was shocked, not by the absence of a headstone, but by the reality of my grandfather's grave marked with a metal Star of David.

'I never organised a headstone,' Mum said, embarrassed. 'I don't really know why. I think I should have.'

Today, when I arrive at my parents' townhouse to collect Mum, Dad says he wants to come too. He's in his walking shoes, his hands firmly in his jacket pockets.

Mum's pale in a white embroidered shirt, almost ghost-like. I look to her to see if she's okay with the shared outing. I know my parents sometimes need a break from each other. But she's inscrutable. Her eyes, often rheumy and pooled with unwelcome tears, are invisible behind glasses that have turned dark in the bright sunshine. She's already easing herself into the passenger seat next to me, a map of the cemetery in her hand. My father waits for her to get in, closes the door for her, and climbs into the back seat.

'Karori Cemetery is very interesting,' he says to me as we drive the short distance to its gates. 'There are a lot of Polish graves. Have you been there?' I have been there, but I've paid little attention to the headstones. It's a leafy, hillside cemetery, interlaced with paths and views of the city's western suburbs in the distance. Broken and unvisited graves seem to disappear at its furthest reaches, blending into the bush-covered hills. I'd just assumed that Karori Cemetery, now closed for new interments, was for New Zealanders with longer histories in this country than mine. But Hannah's grave is surprisingly easy to find. The Jewish section is close to the main entrance, its headstones impressively ornate and old, not far from the central red brick crematorium.

Mum levers herself between two chalky headstones, resting her hand on one. 'Here it is, here it is,' she says. 'Look at that.' She's right. Her grandmother's headstone, unlike her father's, is a large and elegant memorial, the lettering still clear and bold.

'In Loving Memory of Hannah Zam,' I read. 'Died 10th January, 1935, aged 75 years.' Above the English text is indecipherable Hebrew script.

'She died two months after I was born,' Mum says, her hand still resting on the headstone. 'I wonder if that's why I was born down here in Wellington. Maybe my parents were living with her for a while.' I take a picture of Mum with my phone. She's smiling weakly at me behind her dark glasses in the bright sun. When I check the image on the screen, my mother looks bleached and over-exposed: white shirt, white hair, white stone.

Then Dad walks up the path towards us, his hands still in his pockets. He's been at the Polish graves, he says, further down the road. I hadn't noticed he'd gone.

'Very interesting, the Polish graves,' he says. And then he remembers why we are here, and turns to my mother.

'So,' he says. 'Did you find it?'

~

It's not clear whether my father knew the full extent of my mother's dysfunctional family background, but his inability to cope with it became apparent early in their relationship. Shortly after he asked my mother to marry him, Stefan met his future father-in-law, Joseph, who had been weakened by a number of strokes and was living at the Salvation Army home in Parnell. Olga introduced them at the home and Joseph, frail and birdlike, had accepted Stefan's offered hand but said nothing.

'He only smirked at me, liked this,' Dad says, with an exaggerated wince.

When I ask Mum what Joseph had thought of his daughter's new Polish fiancé, she smiles. Her father had waited until Stefan had left before he'd said anything. 'Then he said to me: "And how much does he drink?"' We laugh; Joseph had a good sense of humour, Mum says.

When Joseph's health deteriorated, he was moved to Auckland Hospital. Olga had visited him late one night and realised he was not improving. 'They had him in a room with a red light above the door,' she says. Joseph had asked her to light a cigarette for him when she'd arrived, which she did—'and it was the last puff on a cigarette I ever had,' Mum says. Then he'd tried to climb out of bed, the cigarette still between his fingers.

'I'm getting out of here,' he told his daughter.

He died later that night, five weeks before the wedding.

At that time, Stefan was in the Bay of Plenty. He'd been working at Kinleith and living in the Board Mills flat that he would soon be sharing with his new bride. The death of his future father-in-law was untimely, but Olga's reaction was worse: she phoned, begging him to come to Auckland for the funeral. Her father's Jewish relatives, including Joseph's sister Liza from Wellington, had arrived. They were strangers to my mother, and they had taken over the funeral arrangements. Olga was distraught and unsupported. But Stefan told her he was working; he hadn't really known her father anyway. She would be fine without him.

My father still can't explain why he wouldn't go to Auckland. He didn't know Joseph, he repeats to me. He had to work. But in the seat across from us at their sunny dining table, my mother splutters.

'You knew me,' she says. 'You could have supported me.'

And then she addresses me in a quiet aside that my father either doesn't hear or chooses to ignore. 'It's because it was Jewish, the funeral,' she says. 'That's why he didn't come.'

~

My grandfather's funeral went ahead and so did my parents' wedding. They were married at St Benedict's Church in Auckland, on 30 March 1959. Once again, my mother's Jewishness cast a small shadow over the planning; they couldn't be married at St Benedict's unless she signed a form agreeing her children would be brought up Roman Catholic. My mother, perhaps feeling more Christian than Jewish after the stress of her father's funeral, was happy to comply.

It was a small affair. Mum had a few friends in attendance, no family. My father, though, had as many of his Wiśniewski siblings as could be gathered. Alina and Iza, his two youngest and inseparable sisters, were accompanied by their Polish fiancés, Bolek and Mietek. Kazik, too, came with his new wife, Barbara, who was heavily pregnant with their daughter, my cousin Alicja. Czesiek arrived on his own from Wellington, where his wife had just given birth to their eldest son. There's only one photo from the wedding that features Hela and her new husband Henek. They are standing behind the bride and groom and are barely visible in the gloom of the church doorway. Hela is wearing a white blouse, buttoned high on her throat, and a hat with an undersized brim. She looks pale and tense. Henek, already bald and out of place in this fashionable young group, is smiling weakly. At the centre of the photograph, my mother leans towards my father, her arm tucked into his, her dark hair cropped and wavy under a short, white veil. My father, in a dark suit and tie, smiles broadly, his brown fringe sweeping above his impossibly young face.

After the church ceremony the small wedding group returned to Olga's flat in Shelly Beach Road, Herne Bay, where a dinner had been organised. 'I paid the caterers 40 pounds,' Mum says, 'and I took the curtains down in the living room and washed them.' The couple honeymooned in a lakeside hotel in Rotorua and then drove to nearby Whakatane, to a mattress on the floor in their almost empty upstairs flat.

'I had some of my father's furniture,' Mum says. 'But that was all we had.'

Dad laughs. 'And I had nothing, nothing at all. Just a job, I had a job.'

~

When I was a child, I had no idea my mother had a story too. Our Whakatane household was defined by my father's uniqueness, not hers. It was a relief to me that Mum appeared so normal, so much like the other mothers. She was an enthusiastic cook and homemaker, loved my sister and me to death, was safe and smelt wonderful. She told us imaginative bedtime stories that weren't frighteningly real. My father was different.

Dad looked foreign, with his piercing blue eyes, pronounced nose and olive skin. He sounded foreign too, his accent thick and sometimes impenetrable. Younger newcomers were frightened by it and would stare at him in shock when he spoke. Some of my friends found it funny; I didn't. 'Go brush your hairs!' he would bark at me before I left the house, embarrassing me with his silly take on the quirks of English. I blamed him too for the unpronounceable surname that my peers found so funny. 'Wish-fisky' was a common and sometimes teasingly deliberate mispronunciation. The boys who lived around the corner preferred 'whisky-balls'. Even my teachers couldn't get past the first syllable.

But it was Dad's unpredictability and moodiness, not his eccentricities, which frightened me and set our little family on edge. I couldn't understand why he was so difficult; I just wished he wasn't. He worked long shifts in a job he tolerated and rarely complained about. There he was known as 'Steve' by all his workmates, part of a general and well-meaning attempt to help him fit in, to be less Polish. If he wasn't working, he spent many evenings at the local RSA. These were often long, tense nights at home while my mother, sister and I waited for him to return, his dinner drying out on a plate in the oven.

'He's gone to see the man about a dog,' Mum always said when I asked where Dad was. I imagined a faceless bearded character, someone important, even godlike, to whom my father paid homage at the uninspiring brick building not far from our house. So whenever one of Dad's older, red-nosed RSA friends came home with him, both of them smelling of beer, I'd wonder. Was this the man my father was always going to see? It couldn't

Stefan and Olga's wedding, Auckland, 1959. From left: Mietek, Iza, Henek, Stefan, Olga, Hela, Beverly Jude (bridesmaid), Alina, Czesiek, Barbara, Kazik.

Olga and Stefan, newlyweds, in Auckland, 1960.

Olga and Stefan, Whakatane Board Mills ball, 1961.

Ohope Beach, on a Sunday drive, 1966: Helena, Olga, and Zofia.

be this man; there must be another. This man was so ordinary. Occasionally, if Dad came home alone, the vigils would end in terrible arguments and my sister and I would retreat to our shared bedroom, trying to sleep over the terrifying sounds of our parents shouting at each other. I wondered then what the attraction at the club could have been for my father. What was worth sacrificing family peace for? Was it the conversation? Surely not: we lived in a town where few people understood— or were interested in—his past. Was it the snooker tables? Or was it simply, and more scarily, that he didn't want to spend the evenings with us?

~

My father had no time—or, I suppose now, money—for the things that I thought signalled success in the town we lived in. As I grew, I envied my friends' store-bought clothes, houses with colour TVs and shagpile carpets. Dad didn't seem to notice them. The perfect target for my consumer angst was our family car, a grey Hillman Super Minx station wagon.

Few memories from my childhood aren't linked in some way with the wagon that was bought—'brand new', Dad still says proudly—in 1964, the year my sister was born. I knew every inch of that vehicle's back seat and its red vinyl interior. I knew the best way for Zofia and me to arrange our skinny legs so that we could sleep along its length and how many chewing gum packets could be stored in the ashtrays on the doors. I knew that Sunday drives meant long hours watching the sleep-flattened back of my mother's head, boredom alleviated only by picnics arranged on the Hillman's flip-out boot. By the time I turned 15, when I learned to drive using its clunky column-shift gears and temperamental clutch in the local supermarket car park, the Hillman's ugly outline had come to represent everything I loathed about my life in Whakatane. So when it was sold to a local surfer for $200 soon after I left home in the early 1980s, I wasn't sad to see it go. But for years after it was sold, after I had left, and on my return visits home, I kept looking for the Hillman on local streets, wondering if it would appear, a shoebox-shaped ghost from the past. Who knows how much longer it kept vigil for its new owners on those Bay of Plenty beaches?

The Hillman's longevity was due partly to the era in which it was built. Like so many things in the 60s and 70s, cars were designed to last. But my father's determined handyman efforts were also to blame. He worked on its maintenance on weekends and between work shifts in what seemed an endless cycle of repair. Sometimes he'd be head first under the bonnet, at other times completely invisible underneath the chassis. When he was in sight, he'd be in his professional-looking navy work overalls, using the tools set up on a bench in our little weatherboard garage. I knew the aim was to save money and to ensure the work was 'done properly', but the price we paid for my non-mechanic father's thrift was a car that was often un-driveable for long periods of time. Once, he completely reconditioned the Hillman's engine, a procedure that took a year. The car remained on blocks while Dad removed mysterious pieces of blackened metal, dismantling and then meticulously reassembling them in a delicate surgery. While the overhaul was underway, he arranged to borrow a grey pre-war Vauxhall, complete with running boards and crank start, from a friend at the RSA. But the Vauxhall was even more humiliating than the Hillman; I hid my face in the cracked and smelly leather of its back seat whenever we drove anywhere I might be recognised. When the job on the Hillman was finally announced complete, I held my breath as Dad put the key in its ignition. I didn't let it go until the vehicle was back to chugging life. The Hillman wasn't pretty, but I decided it was my best option.

Our family home produced the same emotions in me as the family car: a confusing blend of humiliation and comfort. The house at 55 Bracken Street was a flat-roofed three-bedroom box that had been built for mill workers in the 1950s. It looked as though it had been dropped on its quarter-acre section accidentally, the twin concrete tracks of the driveway arriving at its back door, not the front. But the two bedroom windows that sat on its blank front wall, one larger than the other, seemed to wink every time I arrived home on my bike from school. I knew it was flawed, but I didn't mind. It was home. The decor and curtain-making was left to my mother, a talented sewer; Dad, whose approach was again entirely practical, was in charge of maintenance, although painting, gardening and building were chores for him, not passions. Every few years he'd erect scaffolding and paint the house, one painstaking wall at a time. One year, to save on future maintenance, he removed each of the old wooden windows and replaced it with a dark brown aluminium alternative. I was initially excited by my father's attempt to modernise our home, but the end result was disappointing. The new windows looked like ugly bruises. I missed the friendliness of the old ones.

Other projects were started and finished only when he had the time or money for materials. When I was in my teens, he removed the unused fireplace and chimney that divided our cramped dining area and sitting room. I'd left for school one morning with our house still intact; by the time I arrived home with my mother and sister that afternoon, a jagged hole in the centre of the living room floor was filled with brick rubble and pieces of dining room wall. My father, when he came home several hours later from the RSA, explained that the chimney hadn't fallen the way he'd expected; the destruction wasn't his fault. The hole in the wooden floor was eventually repaired, but its scar remained embarrassingly obvious for years, exposed in a chimney-shaped gap in the marmalade-coloured carpet.

I have no idea how my mother felt about her husband's do-it-yourself projects; I never thought to ask. I don't remember complaints or criticism from her, just tolerance. Unlike me, she didn't seem to be embarrassed to invite friends to visit; she simply arranged pot plants and furniture to hide the gaps in the carpet. Her husband's DIY foibles—just like his religious faith and devotion to his Polish siblings and their shared, sad past—were things she could live with. She didn't understand the experiences that had given rise to them, but she accepted the results with what appeared to me to be a puzzling bigheartedness. It never occurred to me then that her generosity might have masked other gaps she was eager to fill.

~

'Family is the most important,' Dad would tell my sister and me repeatedly. 'You must never forget that.'

I assumed my father was referring not to us, but to his 'real' family—his Polish brothers and sisters—when he said this. It was clear that he loved them all—but the sibling he was most comfortable with was Kazik, my gentle and smiling uncle. Kazik lived with his young family in Auckland and whenever he and his wife Barbara visited us, or we drove to Auckland to stay with them, my father became a better, more Polish version of himself. He and Kazik were an exclusive two-man party, happy in each other's company. They drank vodka shots with beer chasers, talking and singing songs with recognisable tunes but indecipherable Polish lyrics until late at night. In the meantime, my mother, sister and I gravitated towards the other Kiwis in the household. We didn't mind that our lack of Polish meant we couldn't join in the male festivities.

Mum was happy in the company of Aunty Barbara, her

one non-Polish sister-in-law; my sister and I loved our aunt's energetic and extroverted personality and her affection for us. I also envied my cousins—Alicja and her younger brothers Jon, Stefan and Tony—for the sociable and noisy house they lived in. We swam, ate, camped, played guitar and card games; we bickered, laughed, sulked and poked fun, fought over dishwashing turns and flicked each other with damp tea towels. Zofia and I flirted with their good-looking friends. But always there, at every family milestone or holiday, like the low-key backdrop to a film of my teenage years, were the adults. At the dining table, a plate of salami and cubed cheese between them, sat my father and my uncle drinking beer and talking loudly in Polish. In the kitchen, sipping their own drinks and swapping stories in a language their husbands preferred not to use, were my mother and my aunt. To a stranger, the cultural gulf between the men and women in that household might have seemed huge; to me, it was easy, even comfortable. We all liked it that way.

In 1974, 30 years after his arrival in New Zealand, Dad had finally saved enough money to take his first trip back to Poland with Kazik. Józef had died the year I was born, in 1962, but the men still had three brothers in Poland. None of them had seen each other since before the war. My father and my uncle's departure from Auckland airport was a momentous event. The entire extended family crowded the area outside the departure lounge. After he'd gone, my mother, who wasn't usually behind the wheel, drove the Hillman and my sister and me back to Whakatane. Dad was away for three months and we heard little from him, just an occasional postcard. I remember it as an easy, quiet break in our normal routine. Mum seemed more relaxed, happy to be in sole charge of our trio.

When he returned, he was pleased to see us. I admired the exotic ring with its huge pink stone that he'd bought for Mum and the little wooden box he gave me with its foreign varnish smell and its creamy, exposed interior. Together, we pored over photos of Dad with Polish relatives squeezed around tables covered in white embroidered cloths, posing in front of grim churches or gathered in awkward circles around my mysterious grandfather's headstone. We laughed at his stories of vodka confiscations at various border crossings. I couldn't believe my father had been to these places, spent time with these strangers. But the thrill of his homecoming, like the poor quality prints in his photo album, were soon forgotten; he was just as moody as before. He and my mother still bickered. He hadn't got Poland out of his system.

As I grew older, the desire to distance myself from both my parents, and especially my father, intensified. Dad's efforts to interest me in his native language became weaker as my opposition grew. I could say only a few words in Polish, and that was plenty. I had no need to learn any more. I couldn't bear his conservative and intolerant right-wing views: we had loud, angry and pointless arguments. When he was asked to speak to my high school social studies class by a teacher, I was surprised and then mortified. I considered faking illness, wagging class for the first time ever. Instead I sat at the back of the classroom, wincing at his clumsy sentences and poor English, the repetition of the long, confusing stories about his wartime experiences. So I was shocked when my normally indifferent classmates asked probing questions and clapped at the end.

'Your father's cool,' one boy said afterwards. He'd never spoken to me before.

4

our fear
does not rise on the wings of the tempest
does not sit on a church tower
it is down-to-earth

it has the shape
of a bundle made in haste
with warm clothing
provisions
and arms

Zbigniew Herbert, 'Our Fear'

My father has news. When I arrive at the little townhouse my parents have moved to, the new home close to my sister and me and our growing families, he's waiting for me. He's holding the newspaper in one hand, his glasses and the pen for the crossword in the other.

'Mum's out,' he says, 'but I've got something to show you.'

He's wearing the white hotel slippers I gave him a few months ago—their snowy toes poke out from under his tracksuit pants—and I wonder if he wore them to town that morning. It wouldn't surprise me if he had. He sees me looking at his feet. 'I like these slippers, much more comfortable than my other ones,' he says, smiling, sliding one foot out from under his pants for me to admire.

He reaches into the cupboard by his little armchair under the window and pulls out his new passport, its cover red and stiff.

There's the Polish Eagle on the outside and the official stamp over the black-and-white photo he had taken at the chemist in the mall last year. Dad looks worn out and faded in the photo, like his clothes. Under the photo is his name, Stefan Wiśniewski, and date of birth: 29 July 1929. We both know this date is wrong, a now-permanent result of a wartime documentation error. It's June 29, not July, he insists. Missing and incorrect records made applying for this Polish passport tricky. It took us almost a whole afternoon to fill out the forms. He became tired of translating the questions for me—'but what does it mean in English, Dad?'—and the document's circular, looping enquiries frustrated him. He had no birth certificate. Why did they keep asking for a birth certificate? He'd told them last time he didn't have one. He'd slammed his hand on the table; my cup of tea had sloshed into its saucer.

'And do you know what else I found out today?' Dad asks me now. Before I have a chance to respond, he tells me anyway: 'I have no fingerprints.'

He must be wrong, I say, everyone has fingerprints. They're natural identity stamps, not optional.

'I know, that's what I thought too,' my father says, smiling. 'But it's true, I don't have any.'

He wants me to believe him, so he tells me the story, about being at the Polish Embassy in town for most of the morning, even though he'd only wanted to drop in to collect his new passport. But they said he needed to provide fingerprints before they could give it to him. 'See?' He waves his fingers at me, and yes, his thumb is definitely stained. The embassy man kept trying over and over—different inkpads, different fingers, different pieces of paper—to get a clear print, squeezing and wringing my father's hand like a lemon. 'He got a bit angry with me in the end, that man, like I'd done something wrong.'

I reach for my father's hand with its gnarled working nails, and hold it gently between my fingers. He's right: when I look up close I can't see anything. His thumb is blank, totally free of rings or whorls. And then I look at my thumbs, where grooves shine like the isobars on the TV weather map.

'And do you know what else?' Dad is excited now and his eyes are glinting. 'They said it was free. They didn't charge me anything. It should have cost $150.' He's grinning and warming the passport between his fingerprint-less hands. The embassy man didn't charge him, he explains, because he said he was a *special person*. I can't help myself; I laugh. What does that mean, a special person? My father stops smiling, upset that I need to ask this question.

'I don't know. That's just what he said.' So we speculate: maybe it's some sort of apology, a belated recognition of his wartime deportation, a wrong now acknowledged by the new Polish administration and tidied away. Or maybe it's something less formal—a simple, easy gesture from the kind embassy staff to an 83-year-old man, someone who's unlikely to need a replacement passport in 10 years. We agree it doesn't matter anyway; it was still free, and he's laughing as he walks me to my car, still wearing his white slippers and clutching the red passport.

I drive away thinking how strange it is that my father's thick accent has never faded but that he's quicker at crosswords than I'll ever be. And I remember I have another pair of hotel slippers, still in their plastic, which I've been meaning to give him. But when I get home, I go to my computer first. I want to find out more about fingerprints.

～

When it finally happened, it happened the same way it had for many thousands of Poles already. My father and his family left Poland dazed and ill prepared.

'You went to bed, like everybody else,' Dad says, 'and when you woke up, everything had changed.'

There had been a knock on the door that night, then a loud and angry intrusion. Four soldiers carrying guns had pulled everyone from their beds, searched the house and tipped its contents across the wooden floors. Stefania, sobbing loudly, was given 15 minutes to sort the belongings she wanted to take from the debris, anything she thought they could carry. Dad remembers his father frozen, terrified—and his own shock at Józef's evident fear. The stress in the household was too much to cope with; Stefan asked one of the watching Russians for permission to go to the toilet outside. Once there, he'd sat in the long grass, listening to the quiet, watching the sky turn pink on the horizon over the fields. 'I remember thinking then that I probably wouldn't see that sight again,' he says. 'So I made a promise to myself that I would come back.'

Dawn had broken by the time the family was dropped at a siding near Brześć's railway station. A train was waiting, its wagons locked, on the track in front of them. Thousands of panicking people—men, women, children and the elderly—filled the kilometre-long platform, carrying bundles of belongings, coats and, if they were lucky, food. 'There was all sorts of talk about what was happening, where we would be going,' Dad says. 'But everybody agreed the only way for us was east.' Soldiers with clipboards eventually began calling names and unlocking wagon doors; families clambered obediently inside. There they found cattle transportation only slightly adjusted to accommodate human passengers. Along one wall was a low bench—for sleeping, sitting—and in the corner a round hole that opened onto the tracks below: a toilet. Another opening to provide ventilation and some light ran around the top of the wagon; it was barred to prevent escape. There was standing room only—'we had about 100 people in our wagon'—and when the doors were closed and padlocked, 'that was it: dark.' A few minutes later the doors opened briefly again and soldiers called out more names, all men. Józef and my father's older brother, Wacek, then 20, were among those called who climbed out.

'Then they shut the doors again. This was the last time we saw them.'

When the train finally pulled away from the station, Stefania was left in the gloom of the wagon with eight of her 11 children. Alina, the youngest, was two years old and the oldest, Regina, was 19. My father was 12. In the dark panic early that day no one had thought to bring food. The family was to survive the 12-day journey east on provisions shared by other deportees and the thin cabbage soup occasionally passed to them through the bars at railway sidings. The mood in the wagon was one of despair, my father says, particularly among the adults. His mother, who hadn't been able to say goodbye to her husband or son, was traumatised and silent. She would have known their removal from the train was a potential death sentence, not only for them, but also for her and the children. Without men to undertake the tough physical work required to provide rations, the chances of survival were low for the women, the elderly, and children in the labour camps of Siberia. 'We were all deported to die,' my father says.

Some in the wagon didn't make it as far as Siberia. Dad remembers the bodies of two children being taken from their grieving mothers, without ceremony, at a railway siding during the journey. He remembers little of the journey itself and has no recollection of his siblings or the interaction between them in the crowded and increasingly dirty space. 'I was thirsty. I know that.' Once again, Hela's face is a shadow. But some on board must have realised the key to survival would be keeping positive. Someone constructed a fabric screen around the hole in the corner of the wagon to offer people privacy; others sang and prayed the rosary. What Dad does remember clearly is spending hours each day peering through a gap in the wagon's wooden slats, taking in the slowly changing landscape as they travelled. 'We took turns getting up to take a look. There was nothing to see at first really, just endless flat land, all barren. They didn't take us through any towns. But when the train went across the mountains, the Urals, we knew for sure where we were going. The talk had been right: we were going to Siberia.'

He wasn't frightened of what was ahead. 'I hadn't been anywhere before, and I was seeing something different.' But he was beginning to understand where the real threat lay. 'I wasn't frightened of war. Only of the hunger, that was all. Just the hunger.'

~

The civilian deportations from Poland's eastern borderlands were carried out in four main waves between February 1940 and June 1941. The number of Kresy Poles deported is unknown, even today, and estimates by historians have fluctuated wildly over the years. After the war, the Polish armed forces calculated that between 1,000,000 and 1,200,000 Polish citizens were deported; some estimates went as high as 1,700,000. In more recent years, historians struggling with controversial and confusing records from the Soviet authorities have had to revise the estimates downwards. The consensus now is that at least 500,000 Polish citizens, 20–30 percent of them Jews and a smaller percentage Belarusians, Ukrainians and Lithuanians, were exiled to the wilds of the Soviet Union.

Again, though, my father's story matches the history: he and his family left on the last wave of deportations in June 1941, maybe even on the last train. Soon after the Wiśniewski family's train pulled away from the platform in Brześć, Dad heard bombs falling. The bombs were German: the Nazis had attacked their former ally, Russia. By nightfall that same day, Brześć and the eastern borderlands fell to its earlier occupiers. Twelve-year-old Stefan, on the train heading into the Soviet Union, would remain unaware of the fate of the city, his father, and his older brothers, until after the war.

The Soviet Union's wartime occupation had been disastrous for almost every citizen of the Kresy and perhaps provided a taste of the oppression that would eventually characterise post-war life throughout Eastern Europe. The German occupation that followed was to put a brutal and permanent end to the Jewish presence in the region. But for my grandfather and his son, Wacek, the timing of the German invasion that day was fortuitous. It was clear the Russians had been intending to execute the Polish men they'd removed from the trains: on 22 June, Soviet soldiers killed an estimated 150,000 Polish prisoners before retreating. The advancing Germans were later to discover prisons filled with Polish bodies. But as Nazi troops neared Brześć, the Russians simply ran out of time to complete the task. They panicked and, before fleeing themselves, set fire to the prison holding Józef and Wacek. My father doesn't know how his father and brother escaped—'maybe the Germans freed them, I'm not sure'—but it seems the pair must have been able to return to the little house by the railway, if only for a short time. After the war, Józef would write to his children about the two cows he had been able to save from the fields that surrounded their old family home. In the meantime, though, he was forced to seek shelter with his brother, Franek, who was still on the family landholding west of the Bug River. The river had marked the boundary of the Soviet occupation during the first years of the war, so Franek's family and livelihood, unlike Józef's, had remained intact. My once ambitious grandfather, who had sold his share of the family farm to his brother and left many years earlier to make his fortune further east, had now returned as a refugee, without his wife and with only one of his 11 children.

'There was some animosity there, I don't know what,' Dad says today of Józef's relationship with Franek. After the war, his father would leave eastern Poland for good, moving with Wacek and Wacek's new wife, Jasia, to Wrocław in the west of Poland. There they were reunited with Benek and Florian, my father's two oldest brothers, who'd been German prisoners of war since 1939. None of the Wiśniewski family on the train to Siberia, including Stefania, would see Józef again.

Stefania and her children arrived in the Siberian city of Barnaul, just north of the Altai Mountains, as summer was beginning. They were weak, dirty and hungry. Their 12-day cattle wagon odyssey had taken the family more than 4,000 kilometres across Russia, from Brześć to Minsk, Smolensk, Moscow, Kazan, Omsk, Novosibirsk and finally Barnaul. When they clambered from the wagon into the bright light on Barnaul's railway platform, no one could stand. 'Our legs just gave way after being in the train for so long.' But they were alive. My father's journey from Poland had been made in mild summer temperatures and not, as in the earlier and much more deadly civilian deportations, during Eastern Europe's unforgiving winter. The family had also arrived in Siberia almost two years into the war, a critical 18 months after the first Kresy Poles who had now endured, in appalling conditions, one of the worst Siberian winters on record. The Wiśniewski family may have been deported to die, but their stay in Siberia was to be shorter than anyone expected.

~

'There's Dziadzio!' Lucy says, thumping on the car window. She winds it down, pushes her ponytailed head out into the snapping wind and yells at him. 'Dziadzio!'

I'm still not used to seeing my father in the street. I pull over while my daughter pushes impatiently on the car door handle, wondering if I'll ever stop feeling that jolt of alarm when it happens. My parents and my suburb, like oil and water, don't seem to mix. Until their move to Wellington two years ago, my mother and father were a reassuring but distant presence in my life. I seemed to manage without them. The eight-hour drive between us was partly to blame, but in some ways the physical distance suited me. It gave us all space, I thought. We could breathe a little.

I did miss them though—my mother most of all—in the early days of my parenthood. They'd arrived at the hospital soon after Anna was born, our first and most eager visitors. The photograph of my grinning and still youthful mother clasping a baby wrapped in hospital white is the earliest we have of our eldest daughter. They stayed for a week. With her instinct for knowing where to help, Mum took over the household, leaving James and me to make sense of the new life in ours. She'd been tactful, holding her tongue when I'd scooped her sleeping and cosy granddaughter from her lap to tuck her into a cold bassinet as the books instructed ('She has to learn to go to sleep by herself,' I said). She'd also sympathised, without reproach, when Anna's howls of protest then echoed from the bedroom. And in the early hours of the morning she sat with me in the dark while I fed the baby, talking quietly, keeping me company.

'It will be fine,' she said, 'you'll be fine.'

My father read the paper, went for walks and offered me advice. I needed to take it easy, he'd say, to look after myself. I knew I had bags under my eyes, and my clothing was deliberately roomy and comfortable. I didn't need his gentle prod. So it was

Mum, not Dad, I remember sobbing for when I stood at the front door of our first house with our 10-day-old daughter in my arms, watching them drive away. How would I cope without someone to mother *me*?

Our family eventually, erratically, grew from one child to three and at each birth my parents would arrive, stay for a while, and leave again. But the departures became less fraught and the chaos in our household more routine. Visits to or from my parents were no longer rescues or escapes but, finally, holidays. The babies James and I had made had become children who could eat unaided, tell us where it hurt, read, write and even surprise us with their cunning. These little lives, I fooled myself, were the result of clever parental nurturing and not just the terrifyingly random outcome of a loose biological urge. Everyone settled into the new order. Then, almost imperceptibly, things began to change again. Adults of my parents' vintage, people I'd assumed were passive but lasting features in my life, began to disappear. The first deaths were unexpected and unlucky. But when my parents-in-law died from cancer, a sudden and painful onslaught that took one and then the other, a turning point was reached. Each phone call to my own parents triggered news of further lost friends. This person had died, they'd say; another was sick, another leaving town. What was happening? My parents, I realised with a reluctance that startled me, were getting old in a town eight hours' drive away. Was I imagining it, or were their voices sounding shakier each time I rang? Were they really happy living by the beach, mowing lawns, waiting for news from us? On one occasion, Mum told me she'd been to the supermarket and hadn't seen anyone she knew. In 52 years in the same community, this had never happened before. We persuaded them it was time; they should sell their house, move closer to us.

My sister and I spent a weekend in Whakatane to help them

clean up. The little Lockwood house our parents had lived in for 18 years contained the last of our childhood bric-a-brac. Mum wanted us to take it home. I couldn't bear, though, the thought of keeping the spit-stained baby clothes, yellowed nappies and thinned sheets she had carefully mothballed. I had my own cluttered cupboards in Wellington, my own hoard of new and equally forgettable memorabilia. So almost everything went into crates for recycling or binning: the chipped figurines of cats and squirrels, rusted school and ballet badges, picture books scarred with felt-tip doodles and missing pages. Dad encouraged the process, helping us carry boxes to the car boot, but Mum couldn't watch. She protested at first, gently reminding us of the significance of particular items ('I remember doing that smocking') and then she gave up, silent. She drifted in and out of rooms while we purged her house of family trivia. The last thing to go was the wobbly wooden dining table we'd eaten around as children; we convinced a local café owner who collected retro furniture to take it away. 'You'll be able to sit at it next time you come back here to visit,' I told my mother, whose face was unreadable.

When Zofia and I left Whakatane to head back to Wellington two days later I was surprised—and a little hurt—that Mum seemed almost relieved to see us go. She kissed me briskly on the cheek and, as we drove away, didn't hover, waving, at her usual spot by the wooden letterbox. It wasn't until we reached the wide river bridge heading out of town, with the familiar murky expanse of water drifting beneath it, that I felt a surge of regret. Had we had done the right thing? I'd left this town without a backward glance years before, and now there would be even less to draw me back. My father, I knew, felt the same way. He had been happy here, but his heart had always been in the flat fields of Eastern Europe, near other rivers and bridges. But for my mother, Whakatane had been the only real home she'd known, the place where she'd created her version of family. The debris of her years there—our years there—had been important to her, perhaps more so than I'd realised.

A week later, on a bleak June day, my parents' pale blue hatchback arrived in Wellington, my father smiling in the driver's seat, my mother shaky and disorientated next to him. Removal men, panting, piled boxes from the truck into the little townhouse and we began the slow task of unpacking. It was all there, everything Zofia and I hadn't managed to convince Mum to part with: the Reader's Digest cookbooks and Family Medical Dictionary; the spatula without a handle that was the only one she liked to use; the wooden figurine of a Polish dancing girl, her velvet skirts still white with Whakatane dust. Everything held, reassuringly, the linen cupboard and Dettol scent of my childhood. I still wonder, two years on, how my parents' warmer, smaller and more manageable house in Wellington can smell and feel like the home I grew up in. Does a family come with its own stubborn chemistry? Maybe that was what my mother was trying to hold on to; why was I so keen to be rid of it? And now my parents are back in my life as if our 30 years of separation never happened. We have dinner together once a week, at my house or my sister's, less frequently at theirs. We celebrate every family birthday with cake. I meet them for coffee or lunch every now and then, or my sister drops in for an evening game of Scrabble around their new dining table. And from time to time we bump into each other by accident or I see them, like today, from a strange, pulled-back distance.

Only this time, Dad's alone. He's outside the liquor store, hunched into his black winter jacket, looking at something in the window. He doesn't know who's calling him and is startled, looks first one way and then the other, up and down the street. Then he sees Lucy running towards him along the footpath, still in her school uniform, and beams at her. When I join them he has his left arm around her shoulders and holds the other out to enclose me, smiling broadly.

'Where are you going?' I ask him. His arm is tight around my shoulders. We must look odd, I think, this bundle of family cuddling on the asphalt outside the liquor store.

'Just going to the Post Office,' he says, 'to post a letter. I'm going to get a tax refund, $150. Very exciting!' I sense the sarcasm; he is in no hurry to go anywhere.

'You'll be able to put it in your travel funds,' I say, 'for our trip to Siberia.'

'Yes, Siberia,' he says. 'That would be great. Siberia. Mum will be pleased with that.' He's not smiling anymore. His arm has dropped from my shoulders.

'What do you mean?'

'Oh, she's not happy with me. She's not happy. Today, she tells me I should go back to where I came from.'

'Really?' I have an awful feeling my father is about to cry. 'That doesn't sound good.'

'No, not good, not good.' Then he remembers Lucy, who is standing close to him, listening. He puts his hands back in his pockets. 'Anyway, I will go, post my letter. Bye Lucy.' He cuddles her, kisses my cheek and says goodbye quietly in my ear. Lucy and I watch him spin on his heels and walk purposefully away, waving one hand in a casual flip over his shoulder.

'Is Dziadzio okay?' Lucy asks. 'Where's Siberia?'

～

The Siberia my father remembers is not the Siberia I picture in my head. I think of Dr Zhivago's black-and-white world: sweeping steppes of icy snow, fringed by impenetrable, uncharted forest. He talks about a mild mid-summer Siberia, a dramatic landscape of vast plains, gorges and plateaus.

Barnaul, on Russia's huge Ob River, was only the first Siberian stop for my young father and his already exhausted family. 'Barnaul? It was a big place, industrial,' Dad tells me, surprised yet again that I'm interested in this kind of information. 'I didn't really see it. We didn't spend any time there, only one night.' Today the city claims Russia's largest munitions factory, as well as 700,000 inhabitants, a number of universities and a concrete Hollywood-style sign at its entrance. But in July 1941, the deportees were taken directly from the city's railway station and locked in a disused cinema. (Their first Russian prison, I think. A new reality, taking shape in an old theatre.) It wasn't until the morning after this that trucks took them to their real destination: a labour camp on the city's eastern rural outskirts, a collection of freshly built wooden huts.

Of the nine members of the Wiśniewski family who arrived in Barnaul, only two still alive remember their Siberian exile. One of them is my father, the other his older brother, Czesiek. It is he who remembers the cinema and also the name of the Barnaul camp ('Vostochny Poselok,' he says, spelling it out for me. 'It means Eastern Settlement.' I can't find it on any map). He remembers more, he says, because he is two years older than my father.

'You don't know your father,' Czesiek tells me. 'You don't know him the way I do.' He's right, of course. I don't.

～

My father and I visit Czesiek at his home in Queensland on a winter's day. It looks, at first, as if nobody's home. His house seems smaller, dustier, than on previous visits. The bricks look grey, not the white I remember, and the traffic by the roundabout at the gate is louder, more pressing. When he appears from a ranch slider behind a screen of trees, his olive-skinned face framed by close-cropped brilliant white hair, Dad is quick to get out of the car. I watch while he greets his brother, pressing a bottle into his hand, before I gather my bag and a pen and join them.

'*Dzień dobre*, Uncle Czesiek,' I say. 'Hi.'

My uncle takes my hand and holds it for a long time. 'Hello, Helena. Well. You look very good.' His sharp blue eyes take me in and I hold my breath. 'I see you still like your hair short.' It's not a question, so I say nothing. Dad and I follow him inside.

Czesiek now lives alone in this little bungalow he bought when his wife, Basia, was still alive. Australia was to give them a sunny and comfortable retirement after a hard-working life raising a family in Wellington; they were tired of the damp and cold. But Basia died of cancer many years ago and today the Sunshine Coast is disappointingly chilly. Czesiek is wearing khaki shorts that sit sloppily on his waist, and a grey long-sleeved sweater. On his feet are thick navy blue socks, no shoes. He walks slowly, carefully, on the shiny tiles inside. He has a stoop and a shuffle I haven't seen before. Next to him my father seems almost sprightly. I have been fooled, I realise, by the smooth skin on my uncle's face, the clarity in his eyes. He is old; he is 86. In the gloom of the living room, pressed hard against its walls, are the blood-red armchairs and matching sofa I still remember from his New Zealand days. When the three of us sit, facing one another, we are an awkward distance apart. But Czesiek doesn't seem to notice. He looks intently at me again and sighs, rests his hands on his knees.

'Would you like a drink? A glass of wine?' he asks me. 'A rum, Stefan?'

It's 11.30 a.m. Dad shrugs.

'Okay,' he says. 'We could have one from the bottle I brought. I've heard that's what you drink now.'

'No, I'll give you a good one,' Czesiek says quickly.

I look at my father for his reaction. Dad had chosen the bottle at a liquor store we'd stopped at on the way, and I'd watched him carefully evaluating alcohol percentages and price tags before settling on the more costly option. His face, though, is inscrutable.

'Okay,' Dad says. 'Whatever you want.'

When Czesiek pushes himself slowly out of his seat to find glasses for our drink, my father catches my eye. His brother has never been an easy man to deal with and he's wary, afraid of upsetting him. Dad's sitting upright on the too-low sofa, not sure what to do with himself, sighing occasionally. We both study the framed studio photograph on the wall behind me; it must have been taken at least 30 years ago. In it, Czesiek, a patriarch in a shirt and tie, sits stiffly at the centre of the family group, staring assertively at the camera. Basia is next to him, smiling. Between them, arranged in a gentle arc around their parents, are my five teenage cousins. All have families and lives of their own now.

Czesiek returns with glasses. He is happy to talk to me.

'You know, Helena,' he says, 'I'm so pleased that I went through Siberia. It gave me experiences.' He can remember more about those years than my father, he reminds me again, because he was older. He also had more schooling than my father, at least two years more. But the bravado I remember has lost some of its punch. Today, Czesiek is hesitant. It's not that he's confused; it's just that the words won't always come when he wants them to. There are mid-sentence silences as he tries to recall the places they went to, the names of the people, the collective farms. He brushes off my father's helpful suggestions in these silences. 'Let it be, Stefan. Let it be.' He's right: the words do come, eventually. He turns to me to explain. 'You know my mind is not as good. Sometimes it's like there is a word in front of me and another word in my mind and I can't find which is the right one.'

Over lunch—meat from Czesiek's fridge, cold rye toast and slices of capsicum and halved radishes—we discuss the bush turkey that's moved into his backyard. The bird has built a nest, the large and very neat pile of leaves beyond the window that I'd thought until now was the result of my uncle's own gardening efforts. Czesiek has tried using engine oil on the nest as a deterrent, but the bird keeps coming back. Then, as if our discussion is its cue, the turkey appears, a mud-coloured rooster with a vulture's head, scratching boldly at the patchy lawn while we watch. 'Bloody thing,' my uncle snarls, as if enraged by its timing. 'I have to get more engine oil.' It seems this bird, his nonchalant nemesis, has changed the mood of our gathering for the worse. Czesiek groans as if it's too much to think about. I wonder if the turkey has already won the battle.

As we are leaving, Czesiek doesn't ask where we are going. There's no suggestion of a return visit. 'You know, Helena, it's good to be alive,' he says. He waves goodbye from the ranch slider, smiling, his feet still encased in his thick navy socks.

As I drive away, I wonder about the awkwardness of that visit. Perhaps it was the hollowness of the little house, the way my uncle—still the proud and defiant man I remembered—seemed nonetheless diminished by his age. I think Dad felt the same. 'Can we pull over?' he says a few minutes down the road. 'I need to find a toilet.'

'Why didn't you go at Czesiek's?'

'I don't know,' he says, climbing out of the car. 'I didn't want to go there.'

Later that evening, I hear my father talking to my mother on the phone. Dad has taken the phone to his bedroom, but I can hear his voice clearly through the thin wall between us. 'It wasn't too bad,' he is saying. 'I'm glad I went.' And then, as if he needs to explain the visit further: 'I think Helena was pleased I was there.'

～

The farms around the Barnaul camp were vast collectives, *kolkhozy*, run by local labour. They were 'thousands of acres', Dad tells me, of potato crops, cornfields, and golden sunflowers. The camp itself was less colourful. Along with a number of other Polish and some Lithuanian deportees, Stefania and her children were housed in one of its simple wooden buildings. They had a small room of their own to squeeze into and were able to come and go during the day provided they were back for roll call in the evening. It was a prison that seemed to involve little physical confinement but plenty of misery. There was access to a communal kitchen at one end of the barracks, but no food.

'They gave us nothing to eat,' Dad says. He wants to explain it to me, the hunger, this thing I've never experienced the way he has. 'It was constant, unrelenting. Not just one or two days and then you have something to eat. But you wake up hungry, go to bed hungry and you go like that week by week, month by month. It's the most horrible thing that you can imagine.' Then his voice trails away for a moment. I remember him telling me when I was a child how he'd made a deal with God when he was in Russia. If God gave him enough bread to eat, he would remain a faithful and devoted Catholic for the rest of his life. This made perfect sense to me at the time. *Give us this day our daily bread.* It's the deal I would have made too, I remember thinking, and clear evidence that God must have been listening to his prayers.

With the other Poles at the camp, Stefania worked to earn a bread ration building a nearby railway. 'Can you believe this?' my father says, still horrified by the memory of his mother's transformation from homemaker to forced labourer. 'My mother has had 11 children, she's starving, and she's lifting railway sleepers.' But her ration wasn't enough and any local currency they had was worthless. There was nothing to buy. The Poles understood now how desperate their new situation was:

the locals they met were happy to remind them that they would die in Siberia, that they would not go back to Poland. But life in Siberia was harsh for everyone, not just those in prison. 'We were taken there as slave labour, but then the whole population of Russia was operating under the same system. We just had less freedom.' The few goods the Polish deportees had brought with them were exotic and much admired by the Siberians who had nothing, so trading goods for food became essential. Once again, the life and death implications of Stefania's frenzied packing decisions were in the spotlight. There seemed to be little sense in the assortment. They had, inexplicably, packed ice skates—older brother Wacek's pride and joy—'and not homemade ones, but the real thing.' There was also a beautifully engineered Vernier scale among their Siberian belongings, a tool his older brothers may have left at the Brześć house. 'And Mum had a coat. It was useless, too thin to keep her warm in winter, but it had a fancy fur collar, quite elegant. I remember the people who bought it were locals; they were fascinated by it. They'd never seen anything like it. We got cooking oil for it.'

Czesiek says he attended a Russian school in Siberia; my father remembers only running wild. 'There was no point in school,' Dad says. 'They only taught us propaganda.' While his mother worked, he foraged the countryside instead with other unsupervised Polish children, looking for anything they could find to eat. The nearby Ob River provided entertainment as well as the possibility of food. In the warmth of that Siberian high summer, failed fishing trips turned into dangerous swimming adventures in the vast river's currents. 'I nearly drowned once,' he says. 'It was the closest I came to dying in Siberia.' He'd become trapped under logs being floated downriver before the winter freeze and remembers fighting desperately to push himself between them, trying to lunge upwards to take a breath. 'I was lucky. It gave me a hell of a fright.' (How insignificant his malnourished little body would have been, I think, bouncing its way like a twig down that watery Russian highway.)

The most reliable sources of food were the collective farms. 'Of course, we would pinch things, that was how we survived. If we didn't steal, we would starve.' Watchmen on horses patrolled the farms, tasked with apprehending the hungry child thieves who stole seed heads from the sunflowers or cobs of maize. After the potato harvest, the children scoured the empty furrows for any potatoes the harvesters had missed. If they were caught, the potatoes were confiscated and the children beaten with a horsewhip. 'They never got me though, I was fast,' Dad says, recalling the thrill of the chase. And then his voice changes, the humour gone. 'It was shocking, what they did, terrible. The winter was about to set in and the potatoes that were left would just be frozen in the ground. The potatoes would rot while the people starved.'

After three months in the camp, and despite the warm summer temperatures, the lack of food was beginning to take a toll on the family's health. When Dad's youngest sister Alina became sick enough to worry their mother—'some sort of bowel problem, I don't remember what'—they took her into a Barnaul hospital for treatment.

'We walked with Mum,' he says, 'and I carried Alina on my back. I can't remember what happened, but they must have treated her there because she got better. She was with us and she was okay when we got news about the amnesty.'

5

I would like not to be
I would like to fall asleep
and wake up after the war
she would say with her eyes shut

Tadeusz Różewicz, 'Leave us Alone'

The German invasion of Russia had changed the landscape of the war. Russia, like Poland, was now an ally of the West; the Poles and the Russians were suddenly fighting the same German enemy. The Polish government-in-exile, based in London, knew its citizens detained in Russia's interior were suffering. Long and complex negotiations began, presided over by the British, to secure their release. On 30 July 1941, the Sikorski–Maisky agreement was signed and an 'amnesty' was granted to all Poles who had been exiled to the Soviet Union—believed then to number well over a million—freeing them from their camps and collectives. A Polish army was also to be formed in the Soviet Union from among these released deportees.

Stefania heard the news of their release in October that year, a general amnesty on a scale unprecedented in Soviet history. She and the other Poles in the camp greeted it with jubilation, inmates of other nationalities with surprise and envy. My father remembers that day very clearly. 'It was the happiest day of my life. I don't think I have ever felt so wonderful. We were allowed to leave Russia.' But where would they go? West, back to Poland, where war was still raging, was out of the question. The other

Poles in their camp wanted to pool their meagre resources and rent a train wagon to take them south. The plan was to head away from the coming Siberian winter to Uzbekistan where they understood the Polish army was forming. But Stefania must have been nervous. My father remembers she gathered the family to make the final decision, asking each of them to take a vote: should they stay in Siberia or join the others heading south? Only Regina, he says, voted to stay. 'She felt we knew what was what in Siberia and thought leaving was a big risk.'

My grandmother was right to be cautious, though she could never have anticipated the scale of the humanitarian crisis she was leading her family into. A flood of exiled Poles was now heading south, fleeing countless labour camps throughout Siberia and Kazakhstan for the army bases they saw as the only sign of Polish infrastructure in the Soviet Union. The refugees were weakened by starvation and disease and many were only just alive after a bitter winter. They left their Russian prisons aware that they had little choice but to flee. 'I know we wouldn't have survived a winter in Siberia,' Dad says. 'It would have been death for all of us.' It was autumn when the Wiśniewski family left Barnaul, this time squeezed into another train wagon heading south. By the end of that year, three months later, almost a quarter of all Poles deported from eastern Poland had died.

~

My friend Marysia has come to Wellington to put her parents in a rest home. We hug each other over the table at the café just as her flat white arrives and I realise she has been waiting for me. Not only is she precisely and typically on time but she's also, as usual, over-dressed for the autumn sunshine. She's wearing a long-sleeved jersey. A puffer jacket and scarf are draped over the back of her chair.

'I know, I know,' she says, when she sees me glancing at her coat. 'It's sunny. But I'm freezing.' I laugh. 'Give me a break,' she says. 'I'm used to Asian temperatures.'

I've known Marysia since we were at university. We were introduced by friends who realised our complicated surnames might mean we had something in common; we later studied journalism together. She's still strikingly dark-haired and tall, towering over me. Maybe it's her height that usually makes me feel like her excitable junior, despite our identical ages. But today I want to put my arm around her shoulders; I can see she's exhausted.

Her father, the Polish survivor of a German concentration camp, is in his late 80s. Her mother, only a little younger, is another of the Polish refugee children who came to New Zealand in 1944. They married shortly after the war, raised three children, and have now together descended into a fog of dementia. Marysia is clearly overwhelmed by the reality of her parents' permanent decline and is terrified she may have done the wrong thing. She's worried the home they've gone to isn't right for them, but her father, whose dementia is less advanced, won't consider any others. He wants to be near his Polish friends, next to the Berhampore church where they still meet for Mass every Sunday. But her mother might need more specialist care. Marysia visited the new home yesterday and was dismayed to see Irena wandering the pastel-coloured halls, alone.

'It's so terrible, Helena,' Marysia says to me, resting her hand on my arm for extra emphasis. 'So awful. I've been crying all week. We just have to wait until Tata loses it completely so we can move them to Taupo, somewhere where my brother can keep an eye on them.'

After lunch she'll go back to the home and visit them again. On Friday she flies to her apartment in Jakarta, to her New Zealand husband, an engineer working for an Indonesian geothermal energy company. She's spent this morning—yet another one—sifting through her parents' almost empty flat, finding only sadness in the debris. 'Mum's wrapped everything—*everything*—in little pieces of tissue and handtowels,' she says, miming an invisible mini-parcel on her palm the size of a cotton spool, 'and tied each of them in string. Can you imagine? It's taken me hours and hours just to do the unwrapping.' Then she shows me the sepia photos she's unwrapped today of her father from his merchant navy days after the war. He's a young man wearing a uniform and a cheeky smile, playing cards with friends around a makeshift table on the deck of a ship. All his companions seem to focus on him.

'Doesn't he look like trouble?' Marysia says, her voice a little shaky. 'He's got a look in his eye.'

I agree. I remember meeting him many years ago, when we'd just finished our studies. Marysia was living in the self-contained flat in the basement of their weatherboard home in Island Bay. We'd eaten frankfurters and salad in the old-fashioned formica kitchen upstairs, sipped wine from a bottle I'd bought, then finished off the remains of a cake her mother had made. I felt completely at home. The house reminded me of my parents' house and other Polish homes I knew: embroidered linen cloths, decorated wooden side tables and prints of European landscapes were arranged on quiet, papered walls. When her parents arrived home a little later, Marysia introduced me. We hugged and kissed each other. They seemed thrilled that she had stumbled on the daughter of a fellow Pole.

'You must come any time,' Marysia's father had said in slow and deliberate English as I left, his hands on my shoulders. His daughter, behind him, rolled her eyes. 'I mean it,' he said, drawing his face closer to mine, as if he were fully aware of the charade that was taking place over his shoulder. 'You must come back. And send my regards to your Dad, please.'

He'd never met my father, who then still lived many hours north of Wellington. Marysia's mother said she recognised our surname. But I didn't think it strange that they were sending salutations to my father, a stranger. All the Poles I knew—even those who weren't related—seemed connected by an unbreakable bond of ethnicity. I wonder now if Marysia and I also share this, despite our very different upbringings and our separate adult lives. She had an Island Bay childhood fully immersed in the city's strong Polish and immigrant community; she couldn't speak English when she started school at the age of five. I grew up adrift in a Bay of Plenty town with, I believed, little or no interest in either my name or my history. Marysia and I haven't lived in the same city for years and our adult lives have played out on different continents. But it's been an undemanding and enduring friendship. We've always understood each other through our parents.

'You know, I'm going to get through all this,' Marysia says now, straightening her back and placing the palm of her right hand on the table between us, an affirmation I understand signals our lunch is drawing to a close. As she gathers her coat and wraps the scarf around her neck, she tells me about the dinner she had last night with a Polish friend of her parents, an older woman who's been helping her sort things out. That lady, she says, had been very patient last night, while they'd eaten, listening to more stories of rest home worries and confusing geriatric bureaucracy. At the end of the meal, though, she had taken Marysia's hand and told her in a firm voice that she needed to pull herself together.

'She said to me that I had to remember who I was: a Polish woman. She told me that if I ever felt like I couldn't cope then I just had to remember that Polish women were strong, very strong. I had to think about my mother and my grandmothers and what they went through and to stop feeling sorry for myself.

'I can't get that out of my head now,' Marysia says. 'Oh my God, you know she's right, don't you?'

We are both laughing now.

'You and me, we're tough,' I say. 'We've got survivors' genes.'

$$\sim$$

The train wagon in which my grandmother and her children left Siberia was not unlike the one that had delivered them there. The only difference, Dad says, was the set of wooden bunks along one length of the interior—'and the fact that we could get on and off when we wanted.' It became a prison of its own nonetheless. The family was at the mercy of the inefficient and outdated Russian railway system, already overloaded with the demand of Red Army troop movements west to the German frontline, as well as for factory and worker evacuations eastwards. The many thousands of fleeing and starving Poles heading south were of little concern to the Soviet authorities. The little wagon sat stationary for days on end, at empty sidings in desolate landscapes, waiting for connecting trains that never came.

'It felt like they'd forgotten us,' my father says. 'I think they probably had.'

It's difficult to get a feel for the scale of the journey the family undertook. They'd already travelled from Poland to Barnaul, a distance greater than the breadth of Australia. From there it was another 1600 kilometres to Almaty, the former capital of Kazakhstan and the family's first stop on their journey south. I try to imagine that wagon tacking jerkily into the wind across Kazakhstan's endless steppes. What would my grandmother have felt as they made their way into this ocean of grass? She'd made a decision for her family with terrifyingly high stakes. In the world she'd come from, the patriarchal and conservative society of pre-war Poland, choices for women like Stefania would have been governed by the wishes of others: her parents, the church, her husband or, more recently, the Russian authorities. Certainly none of the milestones in her life to date—marriage, children, even deportation—would have required this leap of faith, this wholehearted and risky lunge at survival. Maybe she was already feeling the thudding, insistent headaches that would eventually overtake every other worry. Maybe the day-to-day trauma of keeping her children alive was enough to drive out anxiety about longer-term dangers. Three-year-old Alina and five-year-old Iza would have needed constant reassurance and attention. Kazik, almost nine, with his quiet, serious stare, must have worried his mother too. Perhaps Stefania's teenage daughters, Regina and the more boisterous Hela, offered a little support for their mother. But they would have struggled to see beyond their own misery. They, like their brothers, Roman, Czesiek and 12-year-old Stefan, had been catapulted into a new and full-time role in the family's survival. Somehow they had to find food.

Again, Dad doesn't remember life inside the wagon, nor can he recall much of his mother's or siblings' states of mind. He does remember the foraging expeditions he made outside the wagon. At each stop the family was forced to run the risk of the train departing while someone was away scouring the local area for food. The search was often pointless. There were no shops. Stations and railway sidings were empty. Occasionally they were able to get boiled water for drinking, and they would eat anything they could find or steal. 'Any edible grass, seeds off plants, we'd try it all.' At one stop, next to a little wooden hut in the middle of the Kazakhstan steppes, while the train's steam engine was being filled with water, the siblings discovered a stockpile of sugar beet they guessed had come from one of the local collective farms. 'It was manna from heaven, the first thing we'd come across in Russia that was sweet. We gorged ourselves on it.' But the family's weak digestive systems couldn't take the onslaught and for three days they were all violently ill. 'It nearly finished us off,' Dad says. That experience, though, didn't stop them eating castor oil berries found on scrubby bushes at a later stop. 'They were little yellow berries and they tasted okay, a little bit oily. That was another disaster though. We all had vomiting and convulsions.'

From Almaty, at the southern Kazakh border, it was a further 800 kilometres southwest to the Silk Road city of Tashkent. The Tien Shan mountain range, the vast divider of central Asia, was the backdrop for this leg of their journey, its snowy peaks immeasurably foreign to the Poles yearning for the flat horizons of home. Then Tashkent's striking domed mosques and Middle Eastern-style architecture, glimpsed from the wagon as they approached, gave the family a surge of hope. 'It was the first time in a long time that we had seen anything beautiful. It looked like civilisation.' But when the packed train drew to a stop, the hungry passengers poured out, running through the station and nearby central city streets in search of food. It was another fruitless expedition. Even if there had been food, they had no money and nothing left to trade. The children returned to the train empty-handed just before it pulled away, leaving many of the Poles who hadn't returned in time stranded.

'We left quite a few people behind there,' Dad says. 'I think Roman was one of them, but he managed to catch up at the next stop. Some children, young kids on our wagon, didn't make it back. We didn't see them again.'

~

The journey to Uzbekistan took more than a month. At one point, Stefania and her children bypassed their destination altogether, travelling several hundred kilometres further south to Termez, almost on the Afghan border, forcing a painful backtrack. When they finally left the train, they were deposited at a rural station near the eastern Uzbek city of Fergana. An online travel guide tells me today it boasts 'wide, orderly tree-shaded avenues and attractive blue-washed 19th-century tsarist colonial-style houses'. This Silk Road city sounds attractive, I say to Dad, does he remember it? He shakes his head. He never saw Fergana; the family's journey wasn't over. What remained of their belongings was transferred to wooden-wheeled carts pulled by camels. In happier circumstances the camels and their carts—'they called them *arba*,' he says, rolling the 'r' theatrically—might have been a novelty for the Wiśniewski children, a clear signal that they had travelled further than they could have imagined. They were now in the heart of Central Asia. But Dad remembers only the misery of that final leg, trudging behind the plodding camels on an unsealed track for three days and sleeping in the deepening autumn cold on its green fringes.

Their grimly named destination, a *kolkhoz* called 'Stalin', was, he thinks, about 35 kilometres from the railway station. 'I don't know any more,' Dad says when I ask for details, for a better description of this new location. 'It was somewhere, nowhere.' When the camels left them, the family slept one more night in the open, huddled together under their belongings. In the morning they woke to a new hell: a bundle of freezing bodies covered in a white blanket of snow.

It was clear early on that conditions in Uzbekistan were going to be worse than in the prison camp in Siberia. The influx of civilian Poles from the north was putting unbearable pressure on the already marginal existence of the country's local population. Despite this, and after their first night in the Uzbek snow, my father and his family were offered shelter by a local household. 'They took pity on us,' he says. 'It was very kind of them because they didn't have anything to give us.' Stefania and the children slept on the dirt floor of the *kibitki*, a mud hut, alongside its Uzbek inhabitants. Stefan was grateful for the warmth, but at the same time carefully planned a raid on the family's store of dried fruit while they slept. 'I feel terrible thinking about it now. I was so hungry.' His mother, two days later, was allocated an identical one-room mud hut, one of several in a small group near the collective farm. As soon as the family was accommodated, the older children looked for work. If rations didn't come into the household, everyone would starve.

The first in the family to get work, on a *sovkhoz*—a state farm created from a former large estate—was Hela. Until this point of the journey, my father has trouble remembering his older sister's presence. She is a blur in the corner of the train wagon, a ghostly accomplice in his Siberian food raids. Dad doesn't know why this is. 'She was always there,' he assures me, 'somewhere, just trying to survive like we all were.' Perhaps it's because too many years have stretched between the story and the telling. 'Or maybe my mind just doesn't allow me to remember. Maybe that's for the best.' But in Uzbekistan, Hela suddenly steps out of the shadows, my father's unlikely teenage heroine.

The *sovkhoz* was 15 kilometres from the Wiśniewski hut so it made sense for Hela to stay on the farm during the week, coming back to her family only in the weekends. 'Every weekend she would walk back to us, carrying a sack of onions on her back,' Dad says. He remembers vividly the sight of his malnourished and slight sister arriving on the dirt track to the hut, bent almost in half under her load. 'I don't know how she did it. It must have weighed 20 kilograms. She was so strong.' Whether he's referring to Hela's effort at the time, or his view of her generally, I'm not sure. But I have to understand how important these onions were. 'They were great. We lived on them for weeks on end—fried, baked, boiled—we didn't mind.' (Czesiek disagrees with the details of my father's memory and tells me Hela's sacks contained cabbages, not onions, and weighed 30 kilograms, not 20. They saved the family from scurvy, he says. 'I remember onions,' my father insists.)

Hela's heroic example must have had a galvanising impact on her siblings. Her brother, Roman, followed her lead and found work on another state farm growing maize. 'So then we had onions one night and corn the next,' Dad says, laughing. 'It was good. Seriously, it was survival.' My father also found his own way to boost the food larder. The Uzbeks grew a fruit tree, an apricot, he says, whose fruit they dried and ate, littering the local dirt roads and paths around their villages with the pips they spat out. The kernels in these pips, Stefan discovered, were edible, 'just like a nut'. So he spent many days collecting the Uzbeks' chewed pips from the dirt, breaking them and retrieving the kernel inside. Does he realise, I ask him, that one of the compounds in apricot kernels converts to cyanide in the intestine? That if you eat too much, it causes dizziness, nausea, even coma? Dad raises his eyebrows, surprised by my research, but he's unfazed. 'Well, they were good,' he says. 'It was food.'

Other efforts to boost rations were less successful. At one point the family worked on a *kolkhoz*—a local collective—picking cotton and filling sacks with the crop. 'It was good work for us,' Dad says. 'We all did it.' But within days they had reacted to the pollen from the cotton crop, their eyes swelling and oozing painfully. For three to four weeks, the entire family suffered. He sighs when he remembers the way the misery seemed to be compounding for them, and describes it with bitter understatement. 'It was just another very unpleasant experience we had to go through.'

~

Outside the university library, it's getting dark. I've got an hour to look at two research documents, one from the 1970s, the other from 1987, which could be relevant to my father's story. The pages of the former are typewritten and yellowed. How quaint, I think, as I flick through them. How *old*. Then I realise I was a teenager, almost a fully formed adult, when this chunky document was produced. The 'Polish children' interviewed by these researchers would have been fit and healthy men and women at the time, most of them with growing families of their own, offspring who were first generation New Zealanders like me.

Who would have guessed—I certainly didn't then—that my father's experience was of interest to anthropologists, sociologists and psychologists exploring the impact of his childhood exile? I know he'd have been surprised if he'd been approached at the time and interviewed. He would also have been a little suspicious of the researchers' motives. Why did they need to know these things? Was it some sort of test? What if he didn't pass?

These documents—like all the material I've seen on the Polish children who came to New Zealand in 1944—reinforce everything I know about my father. After 30 years in New Zealand, the early researchers concluded, the Poles had adapted well to their new environment but were reluctant to assimilate fully. They were fiercely protective of their cultural identity and of each other. They tolerated everyday New Zealand life— its values and language—but didn't embrace it. And in the 30, almost 40 years that have passed since those first questions were asked, I suspect little has changed. 'All I think about now is the past,' Dad is always saying, 'and Poland. It draws me back.' But how to explain this stubborn homesickness? As early as the 1970s, academics were able to identify the Kiwi-Poles' 'shock of displacement'. The Polish children were the 'the flotsam of war'; they had been uprooted and relocated against their will. Almost all were orphaned, many in horrific circumstances.

Their patriotic loyalty to their country of birth, its culture and faith, was something they could hold on to in the absence of anything more tangible. But they also shared something unique, something else no New Zealander could possibly comprehend: deprivation, starvation and loss in Siberia and the southern Soviet Union. Only their fellow exiles knew what this meant.

I'm beginning to understand that I'm outside that experience too. It's an odd exclusion: this man is my father; I know him as well as anyone. I've read that survivors of trauma are often reluctant to revisit or share the pain of the past, but this isn't the case here. He's happy, even eager, to share his memories of Siberia and Uzbekistan—and I'm a grateful and willing listener. But the pleasure we both took in gathering his earlier, happier recollections of the Polish years has gone. As each milestone across Siberia is marked on my photocopied map, each grim moment in Uzbekistan explored and recorded, the truth of his story slips away. It's not that he's wrong or even forgetful; it's just that I can't *feel* it. I've become the ghoulish reporter I once was as a younger woman, an intrusive snoop hounding the bewildered victim of a crime or a disaster with my banal questions.

'How did you feel?' I hear myself asking him, again and again. 'What was it like? Can you describe it for me?'

Each time I ask these questions, I get the same response: a puzzled stare, a platitude. 'It was terrible. I felt terrible. I don't know, I can't remember.'

The library is emptying and the dark behind its soaring windows bounces my own fuzzy reflection back at me. I gather up my things to leave. I ask the questions, I visit the graves and read the books. But I can't live the story; it's not mine. The things he gives me, these pieces of memory, are like Marysia's mother's parcels: carefully wrapped gifts, generously handed over, intriguing when wrapped in their tissue and string. Unwrapped and exposed, held up to the light and examined, they are the bits and pieces of a life. What made me think they could be more? Maybe Marysia and I are really doing the same job: unwrapping and sifting not because we want to, but because we have to. This is all there is. Little parcels wrapped in tissue.

~

Like many Poles scattered on collectives throughout Uzbekistan and Kazakhstan, Stefania would have been juggling two conflicting fears. She would have worried first that the family's isolated location—'somewhere, nowhere'—meant the Polish authorities might overlook her family. The thought of missing an evacuation terrified her, my father says. The second fear would have been equally paralysing: if she left the collective, the *kolkhoz* and its food rations, her family could starve. When news filtered to her that a Polish camp was being formed in central Uzbekistan and that the authorities might be attempting to arrange evacuations for deportees, my grandmother was forced to act. She arranged another *arba* and the family repeated its risky and painful journey back on foot towards Fergana. They arrived at a camp at Margilan, west of Fergana, by now flooded with many thousands of Poles from throughout Uzbekistan also desperate to leave the Soviet Union.

For a while, the situation seemed hopeful. The family was housed in tents and provided with basic rations. But then 'nothing happened', my father says, and the camp was closed. The Russians had withdrawn their support and the Poles were ordered to disperse again. Many, now that they had made the move, were reluctant to lose the connection with the Polish authorities by returning to collective farms. Stefania was among them. 'My mother didn't want to go back to the collective, I don't know why. She just stopped close by, waiting for some sort of news.' It was a decision that perhaps points to her state of mind.

After months of physical misery, of raised and dashed hopes, Stefania appeared to be giving up. My father recalls signs this may have been the case—and his fear at her despair. 'I would see her just sitting and staring into space. It was the worst time.'

Not being on the *kolkhoz*, the family had no food. At one point, they ate nothing for seven days. 'We had absolutely nothing to eat there. We were desperate. We were boiling grasses that we found.' My father remembers the distended belly he had at that time and Czesiek recalls six-year-old Iza 'lying on her back, not moving, her stomach all blown up. Her eyes were so big.' They also remember the lice, 'little yellow things' that lived everywhere, in clothing and bedding and hair, an irritation that the family—all the refugees—had very early on in their exile given up trying to fight. It was the lice infestation that proved most lethal in Uzbekistan. Lice transmitted the typhus that soon reached epidemic proportions among the starving refugee Poles. 'People were dying everywhere, from typhus,' Dad says. 'They dug trenches and were putting the bodies in every day, so many bodies, just on top of each other.'

Then news came that the Polish army was being formed. For Roman and Regina, who were old enough to enlist, joining was the only sensible decision. They would receive both accommodation and food. Their departure would not only take the pressure off Stefania, but it would also allow them to help the family. Every Pole enlisting in Uzbekistan was a hardened survivor, and every soldier who needed to passed on food rations to starving family members nearby. When a Polish cadet force, *Junaki*, was formed several weeks later, 15-year-old Czesiek also applied and enlisted. ('It was 26 February 1942,' my uncle tells me proudly.) His rations, like Regina's and Roman's, were shared with his grateful family. Dad remembers visiting the camp at regular intervals to collect these parcels—mostly *suchary*, block-like lumps of dried bread—from his enlisted siblings. Unwittingly, and in desperation, thousands of civilian Poles were turning the military camps into refugee feeding stations.

When the Polish cadets announced another intake two weeks after the first, my 13-year-old father asked his mother for permission to apply. 'She gave me her blessing,' he says, formally, as if he needs to justify his request to me. 'I had to do whatever I could to stay alive, she told me.' He lied about his age to the officials and, when challenged, was able to say truthfully that he had no papers to confirm his birthdate. 'So they let me in. But it was a terrible decision for me to make. I felt like I was deserting my mother and my brothers and sisters. I thought maybe it would be the last time I'd see them.'

His concern for his family was soon overwhelmed by the demands of army life. All the cadets were issued with surplus British army uniforms—'greatcoats, trousers, helmets, ammunition belts, none of it would fit me.' Anything that stayed on, he wore; the rest he ignored. The officers imposed a tough physical regimen on the new cadets, making no allowances for their emaciated teenage bodies. My undersized and underage father struggled. Dad remembers how the intense drills and marching were rigorous and exhausting, 'worse than prison, I think.' And despite the welcome food rations in the army (also hoarded and shared with his family), his health initially deteriorated rather than improved. He suffered a bout of dysentery and remembers staggering repeatedly from his tent to the outdoor trench they used as a latrine. ('Czesiek must have seen me. He still talks about me shitting blood. You know, some people used to fall into that trench, they were too weak to crawl out.') And then another mysterious illness struck, one he thought was going to kill him. 'I lost all my strength and I couldn't move. I was wasting away. The boys in my tent would bring me food—I think it was a sort of porridge—and make me eat it. In the end, I knew if I didn't eat it I would die. So I ate it.'

In May, the entire cadet camp was moved. Trains took them 600 kilometres west to the desert outside Kermine in central Uzbekistan and then, a few weeks later, further west. My father knew each move further away from his mother was a step closer to freedom. Roman and Regina had already been transported across the Caspian Sea to Persia with the first evacuation of 30,000 Polish soldiers in March. But Soviet–Polish relations had deteriorated since then. Despite their technical status as allies, the Russians had increasingly begun to view the Poles as hostile; the Soviet authorities were withholding international aid for the deported and starving Poles. Dad remembers that food supplies to the cadet tent camp in Kermine suddenly stopped. The boys survived by hunting for land turtles in the desert sand around their tents.

My father is amused that I'm shocked; I haven't heard about the turtles before. The turtles—the Russian Tortoise, or Steppe Tortoise—were great food, excellent sustenance, he says. The turtles would burrow under the sand at the hottest time of the day, their little humps in the otherwise flat landscape providing the hungry teenagers with telltale signs of hiding places. The boys would take them back to the camp, kill them and boil or roast them over a fire. 'They were delicious, so tasty,' he says. 'We didn't mind that they were tough. But every day we had to go further and further away from the camp to find the turtles. It got harder and harder to catch them.'

Finally, at the beginning of August, Stefan and Czesiek were transported to the coastal port of Krasnovodsk in Turkmenistan where cargo ships, hastily improvised for passenger transport, were waiting.

'It was midsummer and so hot. We were crowded on the boats, packed so tight we could barely sit. We couldn't lie down. I think they thought that we had been through so much that we could cope with two more days. So we did cope, for two days.'

People too sick or too cramped to move defecated and urinated where they stood, others managed to push their way to the ship's sides. 'I climbed onto a lifeboat that was hanging off the side of the ship. I could lie down on the tarpaulin to sleep, like a hammock. It was great until everyone saw what I was doing and followed me. I nearly fell off, but in the end I slept.

'And that was how I got to Persia. And freedom.'

The brothers arrived in Pahlevi, the Iranian port on the Caspian Sea, in August 1942. Over that month, 26,000 Poles were evacuated from Russia; the accounts I read describe the 'human wreckage' that arrived in Pahlevi. Many of the Poles were suffering from dysentery, typhus and typhoid fever and skin infections. All were malnourished and skeletal. My father remembers seeing survivors on his ship falling onto their knees on the Persian sand and giving thanks. But he is curiously short on memories about his own feelings; he can barely remember his older brother, Czesiek, being with him, even whether they were on the same ship. Yes, he says, he was desperately relieved to be out of the Soviet Union. Yes, it was good to be away from the horrors of the ship. But overriding all of that relief was something else, he says. Somewhere, stranded and starving in Uzbekistan, was the rest of the family he now felt he had abandoned.

6

*this is how our dead
look after us
they warn us through dreams
bring back lost money
hunt for jobs
whisper the numbers of lottery tickets
or when they can't do this
knock with their fingers on the windows*

Zbigniew Herbert, 'What Our Dead Do'

In the quarter-acre streets of my childhood, life was better when my father was happy. One of the things that made him happiest was food.

He was an enthusiastic and passionate eater, and my mother was a capable and generous cook. Dinners were eaten at the table, always on a clean tablecloth. We ate the Kiwi meals my mother had grown up with—curried sausages, roasts, always a dessert—but we also ate foods my friends had not heard of and were nervous to try. It was only many years later I realised that some of the regular meals on our household menu were Polish. A favourite was *gołąbki*, cabbage leaves wrapped around a filling of meat and rice, stabbed with a toothpick (so stylish, I thought) and baked in a tomato sauce. *Kotlety* looked a lot like our friends' mothers' beef rissoles, though in our house they were served with a hot side dish of fresh, grated beetroot cooked with a little sugar and vinegar. Our 'cucumber salad'—wafer-thin rounds of peeled cucumber, sprinkled in salt and white pepper, dressed in white vinegar and cream—was in fact *mizeria*. And dull, boiled cauliflower or potatoes were always livened up with a delicious (and, I learned on my first visit to my father's homeland, very Polish) addition of a drizzle of breadcrumbs browned in plenty of butter.

My father, despite my mother's enthusiasm for the kitchen, didn't play a passive role in the feasting. Unusually among the fathers I knew, he was an avid food shopper. He scoured the local newspapers for specials and bargains, and high supermarket shelves for imported delicacies. The fridge was filled with the pungent garlic sausage and salami he loved, Israeli gherkins and oily Russian sardines that sat in flat tins to be smeared on toast for between-meal snacks. He boiled pink and horribly real pigs' trotters, *zimne nogi*, with bay leaves, onions and carrots, leaving them to cool in a glass bowl of clear aspic. These he ate cold, one by one; they shivered sickeningly with glistening jelly, perhaps the only Polish offering I refused to try. I took for granted and never queried his loathing of waste, especially of food. Bread was never thrown away, no matter how stale. Leftover potatoes and vegetables were always refrigerated and reheated, served as a breakfast bubble and squeak, or as topping on the following night's cottage or fish pie. Dad had no patience with my sister's dislike of vegetables and my occasional pickiness. What I couldn't finish, he always would. Discarded meat scraps and small bones would be snatched from our plates and chewed until they were bare. Larger bones, in particular, he'd hoard. He'd suck marrow and gristle from the roasted lamb leg bone that sat greying in the fridge days after the rest of us were done with it.

The focus on food seemed to reach its peak on Christmas Eve. If we were at home, and not with extended family in Auckland, my mother would start work early in the afternoon. She'd be sleeveless at the kitchen table, with the breadboard, rolling pin and bowls fanned out in front of her like a carefully laid-out deck of cards. She'd push the table away from the bench and seat herself so she could see the TV in the living room through the kitchen door. Mum liked company when she had a job to do; most often it was the transistor radio that followed her around the house as she folded washing or made beds. I could locate her by listening for the tinny voices and old-fashioned songs of the National Programme. But on Christmas Eve, it was the TV that kept her company. Even though the sun was shining and we'd only just had lunch, she'd pull the curtains so the living room was dark and she could see the screen more clearly. There was something exciting about the darkened living room and the fuzzy summer heat. My sister and I would lie on the living-room carpet, safely out of sight in the daytime dark, watching what always seemed to be a family movie while our mother worked in the kitchen. We could hear the dull thump of her floured rolling pin in action, the reassuring sound of her effort. She was doing what her sisters-in-law, my father's younger sisters, had taught her to do: making *pierogi*, the Polish dumplings we always ate on Christmas Eve.

The process started with the dough she'd kneaded in the droning Kenwood mixer that morning. She would cut round slices of dough and roll them into flat circles, spooning lumps of the sauerkraut and mushroom filling into the centres. Each circle was then folded into a fat half-moon, its edges crimped together with her fingers. When the sauerkraut was finished, she'd make more *pierogi* for pudding—baby pieces of fresh strawberry and a spoonful of sugar tucked into each parcel. In a few hours, every flat surface in our kitchen would be crowded with trays full of creamy, shellfish-like *pierogi*. They sat in the heat under tea towels, waiting to be cooked, waiting for my father to come home.

We all knew that Christmas Eve was a touchy time for Dad. What I couldn't understand then was why. If he wasn't at work, he'd disappear early in the afternoon to the RSA, leaving Mum to the kitchen preparation. No one knew what time he would be home, or in what shape he would be when he arrived. It was a tense few hours. But we were always ready for him. The table was set with the best cutlery and the linen tablecloth featuring dancing Polish women, the one we used only at Christmas. We'd pull the curtains in the dining area to keep out some of the sun's heat and boil water in preserving pans on the stove, ready for the *pierogi*. Beetroot soup would be simmering next to it, along with the chopped onions for the *pierogi*, browning in butter. If we were lucky, Dad would be in a good mood, ready to enjoy the feast ahead. Occasionally though, he'd come in bleary-eyed and belligerent. My skin would prickle as the complaints started. Something—no one knew exactly what—wasn't right. Zofia and I would spring to Mum's defence, trying to take the focus off her, asserting that the food was delicious, the best we'd had. Then he'd turn on us too: none of us knew what we were talking about; we had no idea, about anything.

One Christmas Eve, my mother bundled my sister and me into the Hillman, all of us silent and terrified. We'd left my father raging, yelling in the living room, the lights from the Christmas tree blinking in surprise. The *pierogi* were still waiting on their trays in the kitchen. My mother drove us, her hands shaking on the wheel, along the No Exit road to the heads of the Whakatane River, the place where the children's swings offered views of the water and Whale Island. It was where we would often spend an hour after Mass on Sundays watching boats come and go. But that afternoon the three of us sat in the car, watching the river claw its way out to the sea, watching other, happier Christmas families climb rocks looking for crabs.

'How long will we be here, Mum?' Zofia asked.

'I don't know,' she said, not looking back at us. 'Long enough for your father to calm down.'

I'm not sure that my father remembers how painfully tense those Christmases were, or how much I hated him for spoiling them. I haven't asked and I probably won't. That annual tension, along with my non-Polish mother's extraordinary efforts to create a Polish Christmas Eve, our very own Wigilia, was simply the way it was. I'd assumed then that my mother made Polish food at Christmas because she enjoyed eating the result as much as we did. Now, when I ask her about it, she drops her voice so that Dad, not far away from us in my kitchen, can't hear.

'It was because he used to get so wound up at Christmas,' she says under her breath. 'He loved it when his sisters made the Polish things. So I got Iza and Alina to teach me how to do it, *pierogi* and beetroot soup. It was a big job.'

Today, my children don't see any Christmas misery in their good-natured grandfather. I watch him enjoy our increasingly commercialised versions of Wigilia, with their tacky additions of Christmas crackers, glazed ham, and gaudy paper hats, and I can barely remember the man whose behaviour was so mystifying to me as a child. 'To think that I was once the same man did not embarrass me,' Czesław Miłosz wrote towards the end of his life, in lines I can imagine coming from my father's proud, unapologetic mouth. 'Whatever evil I suffered, I forgot.' I do know, though, that he'll never be fully reconciled to the stickiness, the cheapness, of our Kiwi celebration. When he tells me now about the snowy, dark Christmases of his childhood, with their romantic and idealised Polishness, I find more detail than in any memory of trauma in Siberia. More than 70 years after his last truly Polish Christmas, he can still recall the white tablecloth, the food, the candles in the tree and the midnight walk in the snow under winter stars. The nostalgia is real: those early Christmas celebrations represent everything good about his pre-war past. Maybe, when he was younger, when I was a child, it was all still too raw. How could our little Whakatane foursome, the cooking from my Kiwi-Jewish mother—despite her valiant efforts—possibly have made up for everything that had been taken away from him? How could trays of *pierogi* and pots of steaming beetroot soup in the heat of a New Zealand summer ever be a real Christmas?

It is no wonder to me that he felt the loss most keenly on those days. He was mourning everything he'd been forced to leave behind. We, his New Zealand family, wanted him to recognise and celebrate everything he now had.

~

The British army officials processing the Poles who'd arrived on the beach at Pahlevi made the boys strip. The uniforms they'd been given several months earlier were heaped in a pile on the sand and burnt in a huge bonfire. It was the last time they were to live with lice. They were showered in a communal tent, sprayed with a white powder disinfectant—'I think it was DDT,' Dad laughs, 'imagine that'—and given new, clean uniforms to wear. Then they were marched though the sand to makeshift tents and shelters rigged from the scrubby branches of trees that fringed the beach.

The following few weeks were blissful. Stefan lived on the beach with his fellow cadets, swimming in the Caspian Sea in the summer heat, and eating: 'Mostly rice, but it was good.' Not all the rescued Poles coped as well. For many, the transition to a normal diet was too much, too soon. The plentiful Persian fruit—mulberries, pomegranates, figs and dates—had a disastrous effect on the starved digestive systems of many refugees, as did the local diet, heavy on mutton. 'A lot of people gorged themselves and couldn't take it. They weren't supervised properly and got terrible dysentery. Others were just too far gone.' More worrying was the silence surrounding the fate of his mother, his sister Hela, and younger siblings, Kazik and the two little girls. The last of the evacuations from Russia were taking place and Stefan and Czesiek would regularly scan the passenger lists, hoping to see their mother's name. 'And then, one day, we did. Her name was there,' Dad says. 'I remember we met them on the beach.'

For an event that must have been intense with emotion, the reunion with his mother and brother and sisters seems lost to him now. 'It was a wonderful feeling,' he says when I ask. But this is all he can tell me. How did they look? What were they wearing? He blinks, silent for a moment. 'Funny, I don't remember. I don't remember how they looked.' He leans back in his chair, runs a wrinkled hand across his face. 'Mum didn't last very long after that anyway.'

Then he stands up. We've been talking at his dining table again, the one bought to replace the family relic left behind in Whakatane, the table I still can't get used to sitting around. My mother, who has been sitting silently with us, senses the discussion has come to an end and starts tidying away our empty mugs and spoons.

'It's too much,' Dad says, not looking at me any more, angry. 'I've had enough talking about it. When I think about it: all that waste, all that ruin, all those families destroyed. It makes me sick. Enough.'

~

I don't recall a time when my aunt Iza's name wasn't linked to her sister's. Iza and Alina, my father's two youngest sisters, simply went together, like salt and pepper.

When I was young, my Auckland aunts lived close together, sharing similar tastes in almost everything, including the deeply religious Christmas cards that sat on our Whakatane mantelpiece each year. Their husbands, Mietek and Bolek, were fellow Polish child refugees as well as friends. The two couples married in a double ceremony in Auckland in 1959. As a child, I found that idea hopelessly romantic and spent hours envisaging a similar future wedding scenario for my sister and me. Like our aunts, my sister was dark-haired and I was fair. I imagined the impact of our brilliant white dresses, the frothy drama of our dual entrance in a crowded church. (The men waiting for us at the altar, our future husbands, remained faceless and inconsequential in this exercise.) I remember my aunts most clearly when they were in their 30s, but I didn't care at the time about their advanced years: they were still beautiful. Iza looked like a snub-nosed and smiling Sally Field, my *Flying Nun* heroine. Alina was a more sophisticated Elisabeth Montgomery, the classy sorceress from *Bewitched*. But it was an effortless elegance, rather than cheap TV-show glamour, that gave my aunts their impact. Even today, in their parallel lives of comfortable retirement in Australia, they look younger than they are. They laugh off compliments and are grateful, they say, only for their continued health. Neither woman remembers anything of those missing months in Uzbekistan or of the trauma that preceded it.

'We were too young,' Iza says to me over breakfast at her Noosa dining table. 'And maybe that's a good thing.'

She wraps her cardigan across her chest, as if she's chilly. Her face, bare of make-up, is clear and only slightly lined, her short chestnut hair sprinkled with grey. Behind her, a two-tone butcherbird keeps a hopeful vigil on the wooden chair on her paved terrace. This brick and tile suburban home on the Queensland coast, decorated with Mietek's roses from the garden and photographs of their Auckland grandchildren, is much too far away from that tent in Uzbekistan. Iza is apologetic, afraid that she isn't being helpful enough. 'Maybe Ciocia will know some more, maybe you should ask her.'

I note my aunt refers to her sister not by name but by the endearingly familiar 'aunty'. ('What do you think, Ciocia,' Iza asked Alina yesterday. 'Shall we eat?') On this visit with my father, I feel—even more than before—the exclusivity of their closeness, their reliance on each other as friends as well as sisters. There's little room for others in this relationship. Even my father, a passionate advocate of family, particularly his own, is on the outside. The trans-Tasman distance now between them all is only partly to blame. Czesiek, who lives so close to his younger sisters, his own Noosa home a short drive away, has long ago given up on trying to share their easy intimacy. He does his own thing, my aunts say. I'm happy with the way things are, he says.

All the siblings have their own opinions about what might have happened in Uzbekistan in 1942. What is known is that civilians with military relatives who'd already been evacuated were given priority to follow them to Persia, so Stefania is likely to have stayed close to the empty army camp near Fergana waiting for approval to travel. It was a three-month wait and the family is unlikely to have had food. I ask Iza how she thinks they survived.

'The one person who would have known for sure was Hela. But Hela was always reluctant to talk about that time. I think she resented that she had to experience that misery. She'd promised Mum she would stay in Russia to help look after us, the younger children. And she was upset that Regina was able to leave, to join the army and get away.'

Iza pushes her chair back from the little table and begins clearing teacups and crumb-spotted breakfast plates, shifting them to the bench behind us.

'Like I say, I was too young to know what happened,' she says. And then, as if tapping into a deep and unacknowledged memory of that time, she adds, 'I'll tell you one thing I do know, though. If your child is making noises—crying, shouting, whining—then they're okay. You shouldn't worry. You worry when they stop making noises.'

Iza pushes the dishes into the sink, then comes back to the table and sits down, smiling apologetically at Mietek, then at my father and me. 'I'll do them later,' she says. 'Look at the time. Look at how long we've been talking.' Then she runs her hand idly over the floral print on the cloth in front of her.

'I don't know,' she says, picking up on the threads of our earlier conversation. 'I think Hela missed out on a childhood, she missed having fun.'

～

'She was a wonderful woman, she really was,' Alina tells me, later that day. 'You would never have known her when she was like that. So tough.'

In the living room of her quiet Cooroy home, my aunt is showing me Hela's old photo album. On its opening page is a collage of the family Hela had effectively lost in the war. At the centre is a head-and-shoulders shot of a grey-haired Józef, her father. Next to him is another of an unsmiling Stefania, a photo probably taken in Iran. Scattered like leaves around them are the children, all 11 of them at varying ages. I've never seen my father's family displayed this way: together, yet distinctly separate. The image of Hela looks like an early one, the earliest I've seen, a guess confirmed by the pencil scribble on the back. It was taken in 1939, just before the war, when she was 14. Two dark plaits sit like bell ropes on either side of her teenage face; her chin is raised and her stare defiant. I can see the toughness I keep hearing about and feel a surge of pity for this brave little girl. It's interesting that this is the image she chose of herself for this particular display. She was not as tough as she looked; we all know that now.

Over dinner with my father, my aunts and their husbands, a generous meal eaten around Alina's oval table, we revisit Hela's unwillingness to talk about her experiences in Uzbekistan, the months that even today remain largely unaccounted for. Alina wonders if Hela's stubborn silence reflected the scale of the trauma she experienced in that Uzbekistan tent. My father says he's certain that the family suffered terribly. Kazik, he remembers, talked endlessly about that time in the last years of his life: 'He talked about it as if he couldn't stop thinking about it.' They were all—Stefania, Hela, the girls—so sick, so starving, they couldn't move. Kazik was the only one with any strength left. He'd make grass into watery soups, spooning it into his mother's and his siblings' mouths, trying to keep them alive.

'I think he was really troubled by those memories at the end,' Dad says. 'I think they haunted him.'

Somehow, though, the family made it onto the train that was to take them west to Krasnovodsk, now Turkmenbashi, the port gateway to Iran. So I'm shocked when Iza tells us that same train carrying my grandmother and her children was derailed in an accident. 'I don't know where,' my aunt says, 'I don't remember anything. But I remember being told about it.' I'm sceptical— is it possible for this story to get any more tragic? In any case, Iza believes they were lucky to survive that too. 'Someone told me my mother had moved us from a front carriage to a back carriage. We would have died if we'd been in the front. Isn't that amazing?'

My aunt, I discover later, is probably correct about the derailment. An early book about the Polish children's arrival in New Zealand, *The Invited*, by Krystyna Skwarko, records a crash involving evacuees at Dushniki station en route from Ashkabad to Krasnovodsk. Though I can't find the Polish-sounding 'Dushniki' on today's trans-Caspian railway maps, the author, one of the adult caregivers who accompanied the children to New Zealand, writes convincingly of the event. 'While the train loaded with Polish children was approaching the station, a goods train collided with it at great speed,' she says. 'Many children were killed and many more injured.'

And it seems Dad's stories about Kazik are also correct. When I phone Alicja to ask if she remembers her father talking about Uzbekistan, she pauses for a moment.

'He did talk about the hunger, quite often. When we were children, he'd get very angry if any of us said we were starving. He wouldn't let us say things like that. And once, when my girls were teenagers, he found a weed in my garden that he said was the grass that he ate in Russia. He brought it inside, put it in a pot and cooked it. We all ate it, even the girls.'

'What did it taste like?'

'Okay. Not very memorable I suppose,' she says. 'But Dad really insisted we all try it. He just kept saying to me, over and over, "That's food, you know. That's food."'

~

Kazik died in October 2010, alone on the floor of his Pakuranga living room.

His youngest son, Tony, visited one Sunday morning and found the front door still locked, the curtains closed and the TV booming from the unnatural gloom of the living room. Inside, his father was in his usual spot on the floor in front of the television, his back resting against the sofa, slumped in the semi-dark. The stainless steel pot that had contained his dinner from the night before was upturned on the carpeted floor next to him. Kazik always ate directly from the cooking pot, Tony told me later. It was something he'd done for more than 30 years, ever since his wife, Barbara, had died. Plates were an extravagance for a man living alone, Kazik believed, unnecessary for the purpose of putting food in one's mouth.

By the time my family arrived in Auckland for Kazik's funeral three days later, the room that had been home to my best and noisiest teenage memories, my father's long Polish discussions and drinking sessions and almost all of our shared family celebrations, was carpet-less. In the centre of the room, on the raw floorboards, was an open coffin on a wheeled metal gurney, my uncle's waxen and unrecognisably sad face tilted at the ceiling. His eyes were closed tight, like a child too frightened to look at something.

My father made a high, keening cry when he came into the room behind me, the saddest sound I'd ever heard him make, as if he wished he didn't have to see the emptiness either.

~

Between March and September 1942, 116,000 Poles—20,000 of them children or teenagers—were safely evacuated from the Soviet Union to Persia.

It's an impressive number in the circumstances, but only a fraction of those who were deported. The vast majority died or were simply left behind in the Soviet Union. Many of those women and children deported, thousands of whom later died of starvation and disease on the way to or in southern Russia, were the wives and families of more than 20,000 Polish army officers, policemen and intelligentsia from the eastern borderlands who were also killed by the Russian secret police in a series of simultaneous mass executions in April and May 1940. Their bodies were left in mass graves, not discovered until later in the war in the forests around Katyn, near Smolensk. Of the civilian deportees who made it to Uzbekistan, many—certainly all the women and children without military connections—were simply not selected for final transport lists to Iran. Few Polish

Jews were allowed to leave Russia. Russian secret police are said to have asked civilians or soldiers to drop their trousers to check for circumcision before allowing them to board the ships. Even those ethnic Poles who made it out of the Soviet Union weren't safe from the effects of their experience. Six hundred and fifty of those rescued died on the white beaches of Pahlevi. Several thousand more, like Stefania, are buried in other Iranian cities.

So what did it take to survive? According to my father, it was desire.

'Those who gave up died very quickly. You had to want to live.'

There's no doubt that the intense nationalism of the Poles—a sense that their Siberian exile was a heroic expression of their Polishness (there's a word for this, I learn: *polskość*)—provided mental toughness in extreme adversity. Essential to this sense of noble sacrifice was an intense and shared Catholic faith. It was God's will, Iza says, that she survived. She, like my father, is convinced of this.

All agree, though, that few were nobler than the women who responded to their exile by modelling and instilling that peculiarly Polish resilience in the survivors. Polish Mother, Holy Mother, Mother. Yes, they were the real heroes, my father says: the mothers.

∼

The Wiśniewski family reunion in Persia was brief.

After a few weeks in a tented military camp outside Tehran, Czesiek, Regina and Roman left Iran, mobilised with the Polish army to Palestine. Within a year, Roman and Regina were moved to Egypt with the Polish II Corps, and both later transferred to the front in Italy. Czesiek, still only a teenager, was to stay in Palestine at a military cadet school for the duration of the war. My 13-year-old father, though, would remain in Iran. In Tehran, he tells me, he quit the cadets. He grew tired of the harsh discipline and its buttoned-down life and decided to stay with his mother and other siblings.

Czesiek smiles when he hears my father's version of this story.

'Is that what he told you?' he says, laughing. 'Your father didn't quit. He was asked to leave.' Stefan was 'kicked out', Czesiek says, for continued disobedience and 'doing bloody stupid stuff.' In the Tehran camp, my father had cut slits in the canvas tents above the stretchers of fellow cadets. 'That bloody idiot didn't cut a hole over his own bed,' Czesiek says, laughing loudly now, rocking backwards in his red armchair with pleasure.

I look at my father for his reaction. He's not offering an alternative to his brother's story. But he's not laughing. 'It was a joke,' he says to me later. 'I was sad to leave. I had some good friends in the cadets.'

Stefania, meanwhile, had been housed with Hela and her younger children in a large Polish camp that grew around a requisitioned machine-gun factory to the east of Tehran. After his exit from the cadets, my father re-joined them, only to be moved, within months, to the lush and exotically foreign city of Esfahan. There, the family was split again, arranged largely by gender and age in various private or church homes along with other Polish orphans and single parent families. These homes, many of them scattered around the old, Arabic streets of the Esfahan suburb of Julfa, were grand and faded houses with gardens, courtyards and fountains behind high red clay walls. Varying numbers of children and orphans lived in each house— some accommodated a few hundred, others a few dozen. But each house offered Polish schooling, regular meals and medical care, funded largely by the Polish government-in-exile. The aim was to get the children back on their feet and healthy, ready for eventual return to their homeland.

136

Despite the dispersal of family members—'there just wasn't any accommodation for us to stay together'—the Persian years were much better. Dad shows me a fuzzy photograph taken at home Number 15, where he lived from the end of 1942 until September 1944. Lined up along the low steps of a deep terrace are hundreds of blurry children's faces, some of them topped with hats and berets. White columns behind the children support the terrace's towering roof, a Polish flag hanging limply from one of them. If Dad's in the photograph, it's impossible to tell. 'But that's the house,' he says. 'That's where I stayed.' His mother lived in Number Eight, with his youngest sister, Alina. Iza lived in another home, as did Hela, who was accommodated with the older girls. Kazik was in home Number Six.

The family met occasionally at weekends, most often at Number Eight, with Stefania. Another photograph from that time shows the five of them formally arranged around my seated grandmother. No one is smiling. Kazik, on his mother's right, looks the most miserable. He wears shoes, but no socks, and his jacket is too small; it's buttoned up and pulled tight across his chest. Stefania looks older than her 48 years, severe in a sombre dark skirt and jacket, her hair swept back. Maybe it was the separation causing the unhappiness; perhaps it was ongoing illness. It seems they all, at various times and despite their generally improving situation, spent periods in hospital or under medical care. Recurrent bouts of malaria were common. My father remembers Hela being desperately sick, so sick that he and his mother went to the hospital to say goodbye. 'She was given the Last Rites when we were there, we prayed with her, Mum and I. We really thought she was going to die. It was terrible.' Dad can't tell me what Hela was suffering from, only that all her hair had fallen out. It is this that he remembers most clearly: his beautiful, tough sister, bald and diminished, dying on white hospital sheets. Maybe it was malaria, he speculates, or typhus. I learn it is possible for sudden severe emotional or physiological incidents, including illnesses with prolonged high fever—and, I assume, trauma—to cause sudden hair loss. But over the next few weeks, Hela slowly got stronger, and soon she had recovered. 'Her hair grew back beautiful and curly,' Dad says. 'I don't know how that happened. Her hair had been straight before.'

My father had known for a long time that his mother suffered headaches, even in Russia. When he visited her in Esfahan, he remembers she was continually taking medication—'powders, probably painkillers'—which she emptied from sachets. Their paper wrappers were littered through her room, he recalls. But he had no idea how sick she really was. Maybe Stefania knew.

'Mum came to see me once where I was, which was unusual,' Dad says. 'I wondered what she wanted, because she didn't really have anything to say. She just started crying. I didn't know what to say. I think that was probably the last time I saw her.'

Alina, too, remembers the last time she saw her mother.

'I was playing on the terrace with some friends and I had a tantrum about something,' she tells me. 'Hela was furious with me for making so much noise and smacked me. She put me into bed, but when I came out later I remember seeing my mother through a doorway, in another room. She was having some sort of fit. Then ladies came and took her away.'

Stefania was admitted to hospital in Esfahan, where Alina and Iza remember visiting in the days that followed. 'Only Hela was allowed to go in, we had to wait outside,' she says. 'There was a beautiful rose garden.' I wonder if it was on that quiet visit to her mother's bedside that Hela made a decision that my father believes determined the course of the rest of her life. His tough sister, the teenager who had survived the unsurvivable, promised to protect what Stefania no longer could: the lives of her younger siblings. When their mother lost consciousness, eventually slipping into a coma, she was transferred to hospital in Tehran. She died there, of a brain haemorrhage, on 5 June 1944.

'We were at evening prayers,' Alina says, 'and the priest announced, "Let us pray for the repose of the soul of Stefania Wiśniewska." I remember thinking, that's my mother. No one came and gave me a hug. I just remember all the kids looking at me.'

Kazik was recovering from a bout of malaria in hospital when he learned Stefania had died. Iza was told when her mother didn't come to the celebrations for her First Holy Communion. And my father was asked to the sacristy at the Armenian Catholic Church in Julfa one Sunday after Mass.

'I'd been altar boy at the Mass and the priest waited until the end before he called me in to talk to him. He said, "I'm sorry, but your mother is dead." I felt numb; it was such a shock. I didn't even know she was sick. The priest gave me some money from his drawer, coins he said my mother had given him as offerings for intentions. He said the money wasn't needed any more and that I may as well have it.'

'What did you do with it?' I ask.

He pauses, thinks. 'I spent it on sweets,' he says. 'Yes, I spent it on sweets.'

Esfahan, Iran, 1944: House Number 15.
If Dad's in the photograph, it's impossible to tell.

Above: Czesiek, aged 15, Polish Army Cadet, on the beach at Pahlevi, 1942.

Above right: Wisniewski family in Esfahan, 1943 (from left to right): Iza, Stefan, Stefania, Alina, Hela and Kazik.

Right: Final days in Esfahan, 1944: Kazik, Stefan and Hela (rear) with Alina and Iza in traditional Polish dress, sewn by Hela.

7

Travel light, for the pass to salvation is narrow;
and seize the glass, for dear life has no going back.

Hafiz, 'Ghazal 49: On Time and Times'

On the plane to Dubai, my father tapped me on the shoulder and waved a fork. He was wearing headphones, listening to Chopin. For the first time ever, as a concession to his years, he'd decided to buy a business-class ticket.

'I've been thinking,' he yelled over the piano in his ears, 'about how funny it is that I'm coming back to Persia this way.'

'What do you mean?'

He took off his headphones, then lowered the volume of his voice with an embarrassed grin.

'I mean that the only other time I went to this country, I was only just alive, nearly dead. Now I'm 82, and I'm eating lobster.'

My father, I knew, was happy, and not just about the lobster. This trip to Iran had been his idea, a decision made after the move to Wellington from Whakatane. He was feeling well, energised. 'If you don't come, I'll go anyway,' he'd said to me. 'I'm not going to get many more chances.'

I said I would, but I was worried. Almost as soon as planning began, the political situation in Iran worsened. It seemed that this paisley-shaped country on the other side of the world had fewer and fewer friends outside its borders. In the months leading up to our departure, in early 2012, I'd scoured travel advisory warnings—don't go, all the official American websites said—

and winced at every media report of heightening international tension. But my cousin, blue-eyed and sensible Alicja, had decided to come with us. She was composed.

'We'll be fine,' she had said, her reassurance an eerie echo of my sister's in Belarus several years earlier. 'It'll be an adventure.'

When Alicja had agreed to come, I was relieved. I knew she was fond of my father, and I knew she was a difficult person to upset. There would be no tears, foot stamping or sulking on this journey—and her companionship would add an element of symmetry. She would be a female ally for me, a foil to my father's intensity and, more importantly, the key to a sentimental family memory. Kazik had been my father's first and perhaps preferred choice of travel companion; he'd been with us on that first Polish road trip in 1988. Alicja would be sitting in her father's seat.

~

She was next to me the day we drove along neat, sweeping roads from Esfahan to Tehran, the route skirting the western fringes of Iran's vast central salt desert, Dasht-e Kavir. The endless pink-orange moonscape of dry hills and plains had offered less and less to comment on, and conversation in the white Iranian Peugeot had almost dwindled away. Only my father, scanning the horizon from the passenger seat in front of me, kept talking.

'See these hills here,' he said, 'these are the same, this orange. And this road, I think it was gravel, but I remember the way it went.' His hands swooped through the air in front of his face, marking out the journey's flow and lift, the shape of its landscape.

In the back seat, I followed Dad's outstretched arms to the views outside. He was right about the orange; it was a colour I'd never associated with landscape before. Alicja and I smiled at each other. We both understood my father wanted us only to look with him. We weren't there to worry about the new, troubled Iran outside the car window or to search for changes. We were there to pay attention to the familiarities, to help him recall the Persia he remembered, so that he could picture himself in it again, a 14-year-old boy on the way to his mother's grave.

'You're right Uncle Stefan,' my cousin said. 'I think I'd remember that orange.'

We'd been in Iran for a week. Within days of our arrival, I'd relaxed. Where was the atmosphere of menace I'd feared? We encountered people getting on with their lives, people who were welcoming and even pleased to see us. We watched them going to work, waiting for buses, eating ice cream and hugging their red-faced children when they cried. Our guides were comfortably low-key. So it was a shock when Ali, our driver and guide for this final leg of our journey, suddenly spoke.

'You must put your cameras away now,' he said. 'We're passing the uranium enrichment plant. No photos allowed.'

Outside our car window, next to this road linking two of Iran's biggest, most ancient and most beautiful cities, was a desert suddenly filled with catastrophic nuclear possibility. Here, finally, was the Iran I'd been dreading, the dangerous and volatile Middle Eastern country I'd been warned about and thought I'd managed to avoid. I searched the landscape beyond the car for evidence of that danger but the near-empty desert failed to provide it. I could see barbed wire, concrete bunkers and—there they were—a few guns, small and khaki coloured, pointing skyward. It was a cheap and scaled-down movie set, the backdrop for one of my son's video games. When I looked to Ali for clues on how to react, he seemed no more preoccupied than he'd been on any other day, driving with his right hand on the wheel and the other holding his silent mobile phone. He thumbed its keys idly.

'Everything's underground, so there's not much to see,' he

said almost apologetically, not turning to look at us. I noticed he was still wearing the same checked shirt he had on yesterday. But my father wanted to clear things up.

'So Ali,' he asked, turning to our driver, 'are they making nuclear weapons there?'

'No,' Ali replied, his eyes on the road ahead, his mobile phone still in his hand. 'No bombs here, just power.' He wanted this information to be reassuring and definitive. My father nodded, satisfied, and turned back to look at the hills.

~

We'd met our guide in the gilt-and-mirror foyer of our Esfahan hotel three days earlier. When we emerged from the hotel's tiny lift a few minutes late, I wondered at first if we'd missed him. In the foyer's morning glare I could see only the shy smile of the shrouded woman behind the reception desk. Then a man in a short-sleeved shirt stood from a sofa by the hotel doors, smoothing his trousers, scooping up his keys and papers. He had thick black hair with a flop of fringe, and his shirt was tucked high in his pants. He shook our hands, my father's first.

'You must be Stefan,' he said. Then his eyes flicked to my cousin and me. 'And you are?'

We explained: one father, his daughter and his niece. Our guide shrugged.

'Okay. Well. I'm Ali,' he said. 'Welcome to Esfahan.'

'Our guide in Shiraz was Ali too,' I said. 'He was lovely.'

That Ali, Shiraz Ali, had been an enthusiastic 25-year-old, a student of English literature and lover of Persian history and poetry. We'd spent two days with him, the first under umbrellas and a wet Shiraz sky. First Ali had steered us through the locals who crowded the tombs of the city's famed poets, Hafiz and Saadi, and then through the city's mirrored palaces and dripping springtime gardens. We'd eaten chicken stewed with prunes in an old hotel courtyard and sticky Iranian ice cream in a dark alley in the bazaar. When we returned to our hotel in the cool and rainy late afternoon we asked him to join us for tea. In the lobby's coffee shop, a dimly lit annexe with high-sided vinyl booths lining its walls, he told us about the difficulties of managing an illegal Facebook account and his struggle to find a girlfriend who wasn't obsessed with make-up and marriage. He was curious about us.

'Why Iran?' he said. 'And why now?'

Because Dad had wanted to come back, I explained. He had good memories of the welcome he'd been given in Iran as a Polish child refugee in the war. And his mother had died in this country; she was buried in Tehran. Ali had taken my father's mottled hand across the table. 'So Stefan,' he said, 'you have a little bit of Persia in you. I'm very glad you have returned.'

The following morning, Ali had climbed into the car coughing, dark-eyed but still smiling. 'I'm sorry, I'm sick,' he explained. 'But you need me, so I'm here. We go to Persepolis, okay?'

It was still raining when we left Shiraz and the car windows had fogged by the time we'd reached the city's outskirts. As we drove north the skies cleared and became a blinding blue. I watched the desert roll past like the backdrop in a children's cartoon and listened to local music on the car radio. In the front seat, Ali coughed, blew his nose, nodded and laughed at the driver's stories. Every now and then, he'd turn to his quiet clients, squeezed shoulder to shoulder in the back. 'You all still here?' he said, grinning.

At the ruins of Persepolis, thousands of holidaying Iranians were emptying from the car parks that fringed the ancient stone pillars, facades, and gates. It seemed that in this crush of families on excursions with pushchairs and picnics we were, once again, the only foreigners. Women in black chadors and sneakers posed for photos with their husbands in front of the ruins. A group of teenage boys, hands in jeans pockets, followed us. As we looped from monument to monument, Ali explaining what we were seeing in his serious English, the boys listened with their heads tilted in mock concentration. We smiled at our followers; our guide ignored them. Ali had no time for the curious stares or requests for photographs. He hurried us between landmarks, tipping his head quickly over his shoulder if we lingered too long. 'Where you from?' the boys called, even as we were walking away. 'You like Iran?'

Later, walking to the car park, Ali dropped next to me. 'You're very lucky, you know,' he said, his head bent towards mine. 'You and your father, you're lucky.'

'Are we?' I asked. 'What do you mean?'

'I've been watching. You have a very good relationship,' he said. 'You respect each other. Most people don't have that with their parents.'

This observation from a stranger, someone not much older than my daughter, was unexpected and intimate. I didn't ask what had prompted it. I muttered a thank you, embarrassed, and Ali smiled, amused by my coy reaction.

Lunch was at a nearby outdoor restaurant, its many empty tables optimistically set with gaudy plastic cloths and tubs of cutlery. We sat under a shady trellis of vines, overlooking a stagnant pool with a fountain trickling at its centre. The waiter brought pieces of flatbread to roll around fresh green herbs and sliced onion and we drank chilled and milky *doogh* through straws from plastic bottles. But Ali was subdued now, coughing into a handkerchief every now and then. We were going to Esfahan; he was heading home to Shiraz. We shook hands on the side of the road at a nearby intersection, trying to thank him over the dust and noise of passing trucks. He would probably catch a bus back to Shiraz, he said; he would be fine. He blew his nose as we pulled away. Our driver took us north in a silent car.

~

Esfahan Ali, our Second Ali, wasn't interested in talking about his predecessor in Shiraz. He was looking towards the glass hotel doors impatiently, gesturing at the bright Esfahan day beyond the shiny foyer.

'Okay. So. Shall we go?'

The car parked on the street outside was another white Iranian Peugeot, tired but well scrubbed and smelling of air freshener. Dad took the front passenger seat and Alicja and I climbed into the back. Second Ali turned the key and the car engine rumbled roughly, but we didn't move. Instead, he cleared his throat and began to speak. 'So. I would like to welcome you again to Esfahan, one of the most beautiful Islamic cities in the world. Here, we have a saying, *Esfahan nesf-e jehan*. This means, Esfahan is half the world. Today you are lucky, because it is a beautiful day and not too hot.' We would visit Julfa first, he said, the old Armenian part of the city. Then we would come back into central Esfahan, walk by the river and maybe have lunch. We would see the mosques if we had time.

'But excuse me, please, before we go, your scarf.' Ali cleared his throat again, pointed to my head. 'You must have it on, even in the car.'

I knew I was supposed to be wearing it; I hadn't realised it had slipped. I felt my face flush. Wearing the scarf had been more difficult than I'd thought. More difficult still was getting used to the stares that came despite it. It seemed that no matter how much of my skin I covered, I was unmistakably foreign. At first I thought it was the blond hair that escaped around my face; maybe I moved with some kind of identifying Western sway.

I'd watched the local women for clues. On Tehran's busy streets, they walked with purpose under colourful, neatly tucked and folded headscarfs, their make-up flawless and lips highlighted in glossy red, their eyes in black. Light trench coats, nipped tightly at their waists, failed to hide either their feminine silhouettes or their Western-style jeans and high heels. There was nothing cowed about them, nothing that suggested discomfort. Even the women in full chador were billowing exotic creatures in black. It wasn't envy I could see in those shaded eyes, I decided. It was disapproval, maybe even pity.

I'd been complaining about the scarf over breakfast only that morning, in the overheated and over-decorated restaurant in our hotel's basement. I'd felt strangled, claustrophobic. It was unnatural to eat breakfast, I'd said to my father and cousin, wrapped up like a parcel. Alicja grimaced, but Dad was unsympathetic. He was preoccupied, trying to spread feta cheese like butter on his bread roll.

'I always knew that wearing a scarf would ruin Iran for you,' he said, not looking up at me. 'I even told Mum before we came that you'd hate it.'

'What you mean by that,' I'd snapped, 'is that my complaining would ruin Iran for *you*.'

Now I felt Second Ali's steady brown eyes on me in the rear view mirror, and remembered First Ali's gentle aside to me at Persepolis. I was aware of my father's silence.

'I'm sorry, it falls,' I said. 'I forget sometimes. I'm still not used to it.'

∼

Second Ali drove us south through Esfahan's leafy streets, across the Zayandeh River towards Julfa. The boulevards were surprisingly wide and, on this sunny Sunday, unnervingly quiet.

Tehran's sprawling reach of roads and alleys had been haphazard and labyrinth-like; the traffic in Shiraz had been dense and pushy. We'd been warned it would be quiet in Esfahan today, the last day of Nowruz, the 13-day celebration of the Iranian New Year. Iranians would be with their families, taking their celebrations outdoors later in the day in a kind of Muslim thanksgiving.

'So do you have family, Ali?' my cousin asked, next to me, breaking the silence.

'Yes, one daughter,' he said. 'And a wife.'

'And you can't spend today with them? You have to work for us?'

'No, it's okay. I don't like picnics.'

We drove in silence a little longer. This was the first Iranian car we'd been in that was music-free; I missed the cheerful backdrop of local sound. The city outside our window, without the usual press of people and traffic, seemed out of context. We could have been in any city, anywhere. Second Ali didn't fill the gaps either. He was distracted; his attention flickered between the road and his mobile, inert on his lap. I guessed he was a little younger than me, perhaps in his 40s, with no trace of grey in his hair, but the skin on his face was slack and pouched under his chin.

My father spoke. 'I'm glad we're going to Julfa,' he said to Ali, 'because that's where I lived when I was in Esfahan 70 years ago.'

'You were in Esfahan before?' he asked. 'What were you doing here?'

'You don't know about the Poles who were here in the war?'

Ali shook his head. 'No. What Poles? I thought you were from New Zealand.'

My father told Ali his story, the reason for our visit. It was difficult to tell if our guide was moved; he was certainly surprised. Second Ali had lived all his life in Esfahan and made a living explaining its history to a now-slowing trickle of tourists.

He hadn't known the city once offered sanctuary to thousands of Polish children fleeing Soviet labour camps. Perhaps Iran was so swamped in its own history of loss that there was nothing remarkable about my father's tragedy. Perhaps our guide had crises of his own to deal with: his tense and unsmiling face made me wonder what they might be. Was it the uncertainty of making a livelihood as a guide for tourists who no longer came? Or was it simply a matter of timing? My father, now happily soaking up the sunny view from the car window in front of me, would be remembering the light, the smell, and the generosity of a different Esfahan, a Persian Esfahan. Second Ali would barely have known it.

'So, you're not normal tourists,' he said, looking at us in the rear vision mirror again. 'What is the English word for tourists like you?'

'Pilgrims?' I suggested.

'No,' he said, shaking his head, 'not pilgrims. No, not pilgrims.'

~

It seemed Second Ali was not alone; few Iranians we met were aware that their country shared some history with Poland.

Our guide in Tehran, Bita, had been one of them. Her eyes had filled with tears when he had told her why we'd come. Fascinated by her reaction, Alicja and I watched her take tissues from her leather purse, twisting their wet remains between her fingers while Dad talked. Bita, like Ali, was my age, and spoke flawless English. She'd once lived abroad with her ex-oil-industry husband and wore her scarf with an enviable, stylish elegance. She was frequently adjusting it, her manicured fingers tucking and tidying stray strands of escaping auburn hair. Dad's story reminded her, she'd said, of the way so many Iranian families had been scattered by the thumps and shifts in her country's history. She may have been thinking about her own future too: her daughter, an only child, who'd just finished her undergraduate studies at Tehran University, would be leaving for the United States as soon as she could.

Bita had planned a tour of the city for us, but we asked if we could first visit my grandmother's grave in the eastern suburbs of old Tehran. This was what we were really in Iran to do, we explained, what my father wanted to see. She had a driver booked for the following day who lived in that area, she said. He would know where to go.

The following morning, Bita stood with us outside the solid iron gates and high red walls of the Cimetière Catholique in Tehran's old eastern suburbs. Ours was the only car in the narrow alley outside; the gates in front of us were locked. I don't know what I had expected. This was, of course, a Catholic place in a fiercely Muslim city; it was as alien as we were. But a caretaker eventually answered our knocking. He was a stooped man with a handlebar moustache and a once-white jacket, and he scanned our little group while Bita explained the reason for our visit. His eyes stopped to take in the flowers Alicja and I held—red and white carnations, the colours of the Polish flag—wrapped in stiff cellophane. Like a porter in a ghostly hotel, the caretaker motioned for us to follow him inside. Two dogs barked from their cages as he led us along a stone lane lined with pine trees. We walked past neat rows of headstones that fanned out on each side, alleys of green grass and tall weeds arching between them. At the apex of the lane was a square-blocked monument marked with the Polish Eagle, a stone cross and a Polish inscription. When we stopped, Dad translated aloud. 'In memory of Polish expatriates having stayed here in God forever, 1942–1944,' he said, followed by a quiet 'amen' under his breath.

The grave we were looking for was just like all the others

nearby. The simple headstone rested on a new, neat blanket of concrete, but the inscription was the same: *Wiśniewska, Stefania, 1895–1944, RIP.* My father dropped to his knees on the concrete skirt.

'Hello, Mama,' he said.

Then he started to cry. When had I last seen my father cry? Behind me I heard Bita, also sobbing. I shifted from foot to foot, uncomfortable about the tears of the stranger behind me, my father's tears, unsure about my own emotions. Dad was now almost 40 years older than his mother was when she was buried here. Did people still cry for their mothers when they were 82? Would I? I concentrated instead on the dark-ridged rubber soles of my father's walking shoes, now dusty with Tehran street dirt, the shoes he'd bought specially for this trip. While I watched, he sniffed and wiped at his eyes with the back of one hand, leaning forward to let the other act as support on the concrete plinth in front. Maybe he was thinking about the last time he was here, when his mother's death was still new. Maybe he was wishing it was his teenage sister standing next to him again, not this dry-eyed daughter and niece.

We arranged the carnations, still beaded with water from the flower market, and then recited the Lord's Prayer together, awkwardly, in Polish. Photos were taken. I asked the caretaker to pose with Dad for one. I wondered then what my grandmother would think about her final resting place in this green and peaceful oasis in Tehran's dusty suburbs. Maybe she'd be happy to know her compatriots—mostly women and children whose wartime journeys also ended here—surrounded her. I knew my father probably wouldn't think this way; his mother was thousands of kilometres from the world she knew and the family she'd fought so hard to protect. He felt a pull to this place that I never would and maybe that was why he was delaying, tugging at patches of grass around the concrete, pacing. Then he pressed a bundle of Iranian notes into the caretaker's hands. Would he take care of his mother for him? Bita translated the question; the caretaker nodded and patted my father on the back. As we finally turned towards the gates, Dad stopped, addressing the cemetery in a loud, clear voice.

'Bye Mama,' he said. 'See you soon I suppose.' As I watched him walk away, an old man in rubber-soled shoes, I felt like someone was missing.

~

In Julfa, the Armenian quarter of Esfahan, everything was closed. Empty, narrow streets led to quiet squares where limp fountains tinkled. We tried the gates to some of the district's famous churches, but they were firmly locked. At Vank Cathedral, the most famous of them all, two workers opened a door to the inner courtyard but wouldn't let us into the church itself. It was closed for the holiday, they said. When Dad began taking photos, the men became agitated and urged us to leave.

The old street map that my father had brought with him, faded and almost illegible on the folds, was meant to help us find the old homes in which the Polish refugee children lived. But the blurry street names on the map meant nothing to Second Ali. Everything had changed since the revolution, he said, even street names. Lots of the old places had been demolished, rebuilt or replaced. We had to understand, he told us, that nothing was the same as it was before. Dad agreed, reluctantly. Nothing was familiar.

In a quiet side street, Second Ali paced and talked on his phone while we waited, sitting on a low plaster fence. He was probably rearranging the day's itinerary, but Dad was impatient. Time was passing; he wouldn't be back here again. He approached two silver-haired men who had been eyeing us, hands in pockets, from across the alley.

'Catholic Church?' Dad said, pointlessly, in English. 'Is there a church near here?' The old men smiled at him, curious but puzzled. My father gestured for Ali to help him translate and my cousin and I watched as the conversation restarted. The words swirled, but I couldn't hear what was being said. I was happy to be warm in the morning sun, a sidekick in Dad's story again. From where I sat, my father looked at home with these Armenian locals. He could be one of them, with their olive skin and European noses, their matching old men slacks and long-sleeved shirts. The Armenians of Julfa had been observing Islamic dress laws but worshipping in their own Catholic churches since the community's arrival in Esfahan in the 17th century. It was Ali who was out of place here, pushing his black fringe away from his eyes, shifting his weight from foot to foot. The older men shook their heads, laughing loudly. One of them grasped my father's hand.

'What's going on?' I asked Ali, when he and Dad rejoined us.

'Your father thinks there is a church that he went to when he was here,' Ali said. 'But these men, they don't know which one it is.'

'We went there, every Sunday,' Dad said, defensive now, his voice rising. 'We all went there, all the Polish children, to Mass, together. It must be open, it's Sunday, and all churches are open on Sunday.' Ali looked over his shoulder, down the street, and then glanced at his phone. There were 16 Catholic churches in Julfa. He ran his hand through his heavy black fringe and yawned.

'Are you tired?' Dad said, failing now to hide his anger. 'You are tired, aren't you?'

'I slept very late last night,' Ali said, blankly and without apology. 'So. I think maybe there's nothing for us here in Julfa today. Let's go somewhere else.'

~

155

Stefania's grave, Cimetière Catholique, Tehran, 2012:
Helena, Stefan, Alicja.

Second Ali (left) and Stefan ask Armenian locals for
directions to the Catholic Church, Julfa, Esfahan, in 2012.
'We all went there, all the Polish children, to Mass, together.
It must be open, it's Sunday . . .'

It wasn't a good day to be a tourist guide in Esfahan. On the final day of the Iranian New Year holiday every monument, mosque and memorial was closed. But as the day warmed, the people came out. The traffic built and then slowed at every intersection; the cars were crowded with families. Men drove, with women sitting next to them and behind them, small children and picnic baskets on their knees.

Second Ali took us back to the river, where we walked first along one riverbank and then the other. A series of ancient, arched stone bridges criss-crossed the broad waterway, making caramel loop reflections in the water. Families occupied every inch of grass on the parks on each side of the river. The crowds, with their picnic rugs, hookah pipes, plastic baskets of snacks, mini charcoal barbecues, soccer balls and badminton sets were amiable and relaxed. People called out to us, offering us sweets, inviting us to sit with them.

'What country you from?'

'You happy Iran?'

'You like Esfahan?'

My father was loving it, being noticed. He stopped to answer all the questions and shake all the hands. 'I could live here,' he said to me, grinning, clearly cheered up after the morning's frustrations. 'This is just how I remember it. You see how good the people are? How clean it is? Everybody's happy.'

I didn't know how to respond; I was tired of his glib pronouncements. How could smiling faces and a lack of graffiti be enough to indicate quality of life? What about the lack of freedom, the scarves, the police? What about the international isolation and the threat of nuclear war? Weren't they negatives?

'You don't understand what I mean, you're not listening to me,' he said, angry now, ignoring the push of locals gathering to listen to our raised voices. 'You're just like Mum, you only hear what you want to hear.'

Alicja stepped in, shooing me away. 'Why don't you go and find Ali. I'll wait here with your Dad.'

Ali, when I found him, wasn't happy either. He'd walked too far ahead and had been waiting for us, scanning the crowd, hands on hips. He seemed indifferent to the celebrations going on around him, a wallflower at a party he hadn't wanted to attend. I asked if he really needed to be with us and told him we'd be fine by ourselves. 'Why don't you go home for the rest of the afternoon? Go and see your family? We'll keep walking; we'll find our way back to the hotel.' Ali was reluctant. Was he just being polite? Maybe babysitting us really was preferable to his family picnic. I convinced him to go.

'Okay, if you're sure,' he said. 'Here's my phone number. Call me when you get back to your room so I know you are safe.'

~

'There's something about him, that Ali,' my father said at dinner that night. 'I don't like him.'

We were eating in our hotel's basement restaurant again, picking at our plates of kebab and salad. Above our heads, chandeliers threw a harsh and flashy light, amplified into glare by the mirrors lining the restaurant walls. I wasn't sure if it was this or my father's easy judgements that made me feel exposed and flushed. But I held my tongue, eager not to rekindle the argument from earlier in the day.

'That's a bit rough, Uncle Stefan,' Alicja said, always tactful. 'He's probably just warming up, giving us a bit of space.'

Our waiter appeared, with uncanny timing, by my shoulder. He had served us both nights we'd been here, stiffly overdressed in a beige collarless shirt with silver trim and a napkin over his right arm. He was a dwarf, so his face was level with mine, the perfect height for dealing with seated customers.

'Is everything all right?' he asked in clipped English. 'Would you like more to drink?' After almost a week with no alcohol, I would have liked to ask for a glass of wine. But I pointed instead to the Coke cans already on our table.

'No, thanks. I think we have plenty.'

After the waiter left, there was silence at our table for a moment.

'That waiter's a dwarf,' my father said.

～

On our second morning in Esfahan, Second Ali arrived at our hotel wearing the same clothes he'd worn the day before.

'How did you sleep this time?' Dad asked when we climbed into his car.

'Not good,' Ali said, abruptly. Maybe he sensed the tone of displeasure in my father's question; today he wanted to explain. 'You know, my doctor has given me some medicine because he says I'm too, what's the word . . . worried, anxious. Things in my house are not good, with my wife, with her family. But the medicine, it doesn't help, I sleep late and then wake so early, and I feel sick, terrible, I don't know why.'

He cleared his throat, waiting for a reaction from the car. My cousin and I exchanged glances, but said nothing.

'That's no good, Ali,' Dad said instead, putting his hand on Second Ali's shoulder. 'I hope you feel better soon.' My father's hand stayed on our guide's shoulder and Ali's eyes rested on me in the rear vision mirror.

'Good, you have your scarf on today,' he said. 'That's better.'

～

'It's our last night in Iran,' I said to Ali. 'Is there somewhere we can go for dinner?'

He responded with a blank stare. Our arrangement included lunch only and he was not responsible for our evening activities. 'I know dinner's not part of your job,' I said quickly, 'but it would be nice to go out somewhere. We'd like you to be our guest.'

The hotel, a multi-storey block on the outskirts of the ancient city of Kashan, had a façade that promised a classy Persian experience. Inside, though, a single mirrored lift opened to dark, sealed corridors that steamed with cooking odours and stale cigarette smoke. From my room on the fourth floor, I'd already watched the red sun drop over the city's low-rise streets, straining to hear the call to prayer from the local mosque over the noise of rush-hour traffic below. I couldn't bear the thought of spending the evening here. While Ali and I talked about plans with my father and Alicja, the manager hovered hopefully at the hotel's restaurant entrance, empty tables visible through an archway behind him.

'Pizza? You want to try Iranian pizza?' Ali suggested.

Iranian pizza proved to be no better or worse than any other pizza I'd eaten. It was delivered on large, flat plastic plates, shiny with cheese, at a fast-food restaurant five minutes' drive from the hotel. What made it 'Iranian', Second Ali explained, was the liberal addition of ketchup, several sachets of which accompanied each plate. 'Like this,' he said, squirting a generous zigzag over his pizza's glistening surface. Over his shoulder, two children were ignoring their own plates of food and staring at us, the smallest of them wearing a scarf of vivid pink, its fringes tucked firmly in her jacket collar. She was sealed, covered, from head to toe. Her mother, also shrouded, shook her daughter's shoulder, urging her to eat. She reluctantly turned away.

'I wanted to ask your advice about something,' Second Ali said. 'So maybe I could buy tea when we are back at the hotel?'

161

I was intrigued, though unsure whether it was our collective advice he was seeking. Second Ali had become progressively more withdrawn over the three days we'd been with him, peeling away from us at tourist spots as if he were ashamed of the sights, ashamed of us. It seemed he had nothing more to tell us. Here is Iran, his silence said, make what you will of it. That morning, as we'd wandered alone through the pink-stoned underground houses of Kashan and, later, through the gardens of the Fin Palace, he stood in shady corners, making calls on his mobile phone. He would be driving us the last few hours to Tehran the following morning in the white Peugeot, leaving us at the airport for our flight back to Dubai. I wouldn't miss his company, but I wanted to know his story.

'It's my wife,' he said boldly, when our tea arrived. We were sitting, facing each other on the vinyl sofas in the empty hotel foyer, three New Zealanders and one Iranian man with white cups and saucers on our knees. 'I need advice about my wife.' Alicja and I looked at each other, suddenly on alert. 'I don't want to be married to her any more.' His wife, he explained, had 'let herself get fat' since they married. He had nothing in common with her and nothing to say to her. He didn't feel anything for her. But if he divorced her, he would be bankrupted; he had signed a contract with her family before they married.

'What do you think I should do?' he asked.

There was a silence while we gathered our thoughts. What was this man asking for?

'Well,' said Alicja, bravely, 'if you really are so terribly unhappy, maybe you would both be better off not being married any more. Perhaps you just need to pay what you have to pay and start again, fresh.' Second Ali didn't respond, but shifted his eyes to me through his heavy fringe of hair.

'I agree,' I said. 'Your wife must be very unhappy if you are living in the same house and you don't want to be with her.

Money isn't the most important thing.'

Then Ali turned my father. 'Okay Stefan, you are a wise person. You are an old man. What do you think?' Dad, surprisingly, seemed pleased to be addressed in this way. He cleared his throat and pulled himself forward on his seat.

'Well, I think that marriage is not an easy thing. I think sometimes it's good and other times it's bad. But I think that when you get married, that's it, you're married. You need to stay with your wife and try and be happy. That's what I think.'

Second Ali put his cup and saucer, the tea untouched, onto the mahogany coffee table between us and stood up.

'Okay, I will go to bed now,' he said. 'Stefan, thank you for the talk. See you all in the morning.'

8

~

Oh we live like the rich
With music at the touch of a switch,
Light in the middle of the night,
Water in the house as from a spring.
Hot, if you wish, or cold, or anything
For the comfort of the flesh,
In my country. Fragment
Of new skin at the edge of the world's ulcer.

Ruth Dallas, 'Letter to a Chinese Poet'

On Wellington's breezy waterfront in November 1944, 732 bewildered Polish children clambered off the troop ship *USS General Randall.*

Somewhere in the crowd of shaven-headed boys and big-eyed serious girls was my father. I've searched the photographs and old film footage taken on that day, but I can't see him. The children who do feature are smiling, nervous, unable to comprehend the welcome they are experiencing. The noisy military bands, officials and locals who cheer and throw money and chocolate are there to welcome these little victims of war. But I know my father would have been keeping his distance, lurking in the background. At 15 years of age, Stefan was old enough to understand what a strange accident his arrival in New Zealand was. He was also old enough to know that this welcome wasn't the one he had been praying for and that this curious green place—despite the enthusiasm of the inhabitants—was not his ultimate destination. It was just a temporary stopover, a place to recharge before the real return home to Poland when the war was over. He wasn't sure what all the fuss was about. After all, they weren't going to be staying.

The journey to New Zealand had begun in late September, two months after Stefania died. Persia had been their sanctuary for almost two years, but longer-term homes were being sought for the more than 3,000 children who had recovered their health in Esfahan. The Polish government in London had appealed to the League of Nations for help and family groups were being sent as far afield as India, others to various British colonies in Africa. Plans had been in place for the Wiśniewski children and their mother to go to East Africa, but they were shelved when Stefania died. Without an adult to accompany them (their father Józef's fate remained a mystery) the children were effectively orphans. Africa was not taking orphans. Different plans had to be made.

They heard they would be going to New Zealand at the last minute. 'We were some of the last to get on that transport here,' my father says. 'Everything changed when Mum died.' He knew nothing about New Zealand—'I just knew it was at the bottom of the world'—and he was wary about travelling even further away from Poland, from home. 'There was just this sense of everything still being totally out of our control, everything just kept happening to us. We had no say.'

For New Zealand, the invitation extended to the 732 Polish children and 105 adults by Labour Prime Minister Peter Fraser was unprecedented and, to some extent, the result of chance. Fraser's wife, Janet, was a friend of Countess Maria Wodzicka, wife of the Polish Consul-General and the Polish Red Cross delegate in New Zealand. But this country had little experience of Poles or Polish culture. Up until the war, there had been relatively few ethnic Polish migrants, most of them rural settlers brought to the country in the late 19th century as assisted migrants, as part of the Vogel Scheme. The country's refugee immigration policy before World War II had been governed by legislation heavily biased in favour of Britons, to whom free entry was allowed, and weighted against Jews and eastern Europeans who were generally seen as undesirable settlers. The Polish orphan children were being offered only temporary refuge in New Zealand for the duration of the war. Their first home would be a hastily converted army camp in Pahiatua.

For my father, the journey from Iran had started on an overcrowded British merchant ship and then, from Bombay, on the *General Randall*, which was taking home American, Australian and New Zealand soldiers. The friendliness of the returning soldiers on the ship was the highlight of that final wartime journey, helping the traumatised children break down their fear of adults in military uniform. 'The soldiers were great,' Dad recalls, 'joking and laughing with us. It was the first time I tried chewing gum.' But by the time the children were on the train that took them to their first New Zealand beds in Pahiatua, they'd tired of the enthusiastic and overwhelming welcome from the locals. Many of the younger children hid behind the seats in my father's carriage, trying to avoid the crowds that pushed against the train windows at every station to get a look, to throw them more money, give them flowers. Dad remembers collecting only the biggest coins—the pennies—that hit the floor. 'We didn't realise that the small ones were worth more,' he says. 'It was all too much.'

It was a wearying and puzzling introduction to the country that was, despite my father's ambitions, to become his permanent home. It was also a day that defined everything that followed. Today, after 70 years of life in New Zealand, Dad is still one of the Polish children. When he dies he will be one of the Polish children. I am a child of one of the Polish children.

~

Dad is waving a piece of today's newspaper at me. 'How Socrates Saved My Life', the headline reads.

'Did you see this?' he asks. 'It's very good.'

I did see it. I hadn't taken it in.

'I like this bit. "Let love lift you up." It's Plato.' He says 'Plaato', and I fight the urge to start a discussion about pronunciation. '"Plato believed we could lift ourselves out of our egotism by passionately loving other people, or beauty, or goodness, and through love we could even connect to God." It's very good.'

My mother sits opposite me, listening. She looks uncomfortable, her arms folded tightly over her chest, her face stony. Maybe there has been a discussion about this article already today.

'Oh, and this bit,' Dad continues. '"Some things are up to us and others are not." That's Epictetus, a Stoic philosopher. "We don't control the economy, the weather, other people, our reputation, our own bodies. We can influence these things, but we don't have complete control over them. The only thing we do have control over is our own thoughts and beliefs." This is so right. This is what I'm telling Mum.'

So there has been a discussion. She makes a snorting noise and hoists herself out of her chair.

'I'm cooking dinner,' she says.

'Mum needs to not worry about stuff she can't control,' Dad says. 'Like Angela Lawson getting a divorce.'

'It's Nigella Lawson,' she says from behind the kitchen bench, 'not Angela. And I'm not worrying about her. I'm just interested. It's better than worrying about everything else.'

'What sort of everything else?' I ask her. 'What else do you worry about?'

My mother looks at me and rolls her eyes theatrically towards my father. I can't tell if my father notices. 'Everything else: the past, my past,' she says.

Dad snorts now. 'Your past is not worth worrying about. You can't do anything about it.'

It's not clear if he's referring to my mother's past in particular, or the past generally. I suspect the former; his past is tragic and noble, it can be worn like a badge, with pride. His wife's troubled family history is seedy, amoral and best forgotten. ('What sort of woman does that,' he said to me once, 'leaves their child and never comes back?')

'It's like what this article says, this philosopher, Seneca,' Dad continues, ignoring the clatter coming from the kitchen bench. '"What is the point of dragging up sufferings that are over, of being miserable now, because you were miserable then? We can go through life walking backwards, constantly ruminating on past injuries or on how things were better in the past. Likewise, we can worry endlessly about the future. Or we can simply choose to make the most of the present."

'It's very good, this article.'

~

My father's much anticipated return to his homeland never eventuated when the war ended and Poland was ceded to Russia. Poland had become an inconvenient ally. At Yalta, in February 1945, Roosevelt and Churchill largely gave in to Stalin's demands to annex the eastern borderlands of Poland and to recognise the Soviet-sponsored provisional government installed in Polish territories then controlled by the Red Army. Poles everywhere were dismayed by what they now saw as the Allies' betrayal. In New Zealand, my teenage father was equally angered by the local joy at Hitler's defeat.

'For me there was nothing to celebrate,' Dad explains bluntly. 'Everyone in New Zealand hated Hitler after the war and Stalin was the good guy. So how could I complain about Stalin? Poland was betrayed by the Allies and sold to Russia.' He knew then that a return to Poland was unlikely. 'My desire was only to go back. I wanted with all my heart to go back. But we couldn't return to the system that had been imposed on Poland, the same system that sent us to Siberia.'

The disappointment and fury over his country's predicament only deepened with the discovery that his father and older siblings were still alive. In the four years that had passed since the family was marshalled onto cattle wagons for the journey to Siberia, there had been no word on the fate of my grandfather and his older sons. The Red Cross, though, managed to connect the Wiśniewski children with their father, who was living in the west of Poland in the formerly German city of Breslaw, now Wrocław. 'It was like a resurrection,' Dad says. 'It was wonderful.' But things were grim at home. More than six million Poles—20 percent of the pre-war population—had died during the war, half of them Polish Jews. The country's cities were in ruins, 60 percent of its industrial capacity had been lost, and a third of its cultural and intellectual elite had been targeted and killed. Józef, now a widower, was living in a flat with his son Wacek and Wacek's new wife Jasia. This was the same grey accommodation I would visit 40 years later. He was supplementing the family's meagre income by selling the milk from two cows he'd somehow transported from the old home in Brześć, now renamed Brest by the Soviet victors. Stay there, my grandfather wrote to his children in New Zealand, if you are getting schooling and food. There is nothing for you in Poland.

Alicja sends me translated transcripts of some of Józef's letters found in her father's papers, and I read a letter he wrote from Wrocław in 1948.

'My beloved children. How grateful I am to God that after so many years of separation I can write these few words to you. I am alive and healthy . . . I hope God will bless you and as a

169

father I bless you too. Maybe one day we can all be together again.' He worries, helplessly, about his adult sons—'I pray to God that he saves you from alcoholism, because it's the worst that can happen'—and about his own health—'I am getting old and much weaker and have a lot of pain in my legs.' His words are heartwarming and a little sad. They are, as Alicja points out, the words of someone who has reluctantly accepted the likelihood of the family's permanent separation. The three oldest sons—Florian, Benek and Wacek—were still in Poland. Regina and Roman, like many of the Polish II Corps, had stayed in the United Kingdom. Czesiek, in the meantime, had followed his younger siblings to New Zealand. Ten years later, a few years before his death, Józef would write another letter to his children in New Zealand, his last—and this time with a little more bitterness.

'I am very weak and don't think I will live much longer,' he wrote. 'The war came and took away everything, even my own wife and eight loving children . . . Nothing is really ours in this world, everything is nothing.'

The hopelessness in his words is haunting. I hold his letter in my hands and want to tell my dying grandfather he is wrong. Don't worry, I want to say; everything will be okay.

~

In the summer of 1974, a grey Hillman station wagon bumped its way onto the grass verge of a paddock in rural Wairarapa. It was a strange place to stop, an unscheduled interlude on a family camping trip around the North Island, the only childhood camping holiday I remember.

My sister and I followed our parents onto the grass in our shorts and bare feet, squinting in the afternoon glare. This was where Dad had lived when he first came to New Zealand, he told us, the site of the camp that had housed all the Polish children. I scanned the green paddock's horizon for signs of habitation: where had the children lived? Macrocarpa trees swayed on the paddock's hazy fringes and sheep blinked at us in the heat. There was nothing to see. But my father was already climbing the barbed wire fence, making his way across the grass, scattering the sheep. Mum and my sister and I scrambled after him.

'What is it Dad?' Zofia asked.

'A grotto,' he said, 'to Our Lady. I remember when we made it, we carried stones up from the river.'

The grotto that I thought had looked like an outhouse as we drew near was disappointingly empty. One of its walls seemed near collapse, and rocky debris was scattered amidst sheep droppings in the grass below. But the Polish Eagle was still there, etched into the concrete on the back, a strange and angry phoenix.

'I'll take a photo,' Dad said. 'Stand there.'

The photograph shows my sister and me staring into the sun, strands of hair lifting across our faces in the afternoon breeze. Our childish bodies lean on the grotto's unstable walls, levered on impossibly thin and tanned legs. Between us is a piece of my father's past, slowly disappearing into history, just like his two little girls.

~

Until the prospects of a return to Poland were ruled out at the end of the war, when the New Zealand government offered them the option of a permanent home, many of the Polish children had remained at the camp in Pahiatua. This 'little Poland' had not prepared my father, or any of the children, for Kiwi life.

The wooden barracks and fences of the Polish children's camp were a relatively new feature on the Wairarapa landscape when

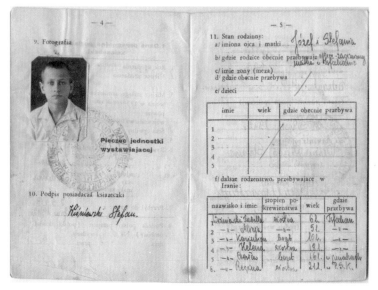

Stefan's identity papers, Iran, 1944.

On the USS General Randall, en route to New Zealand, 1944:
Stefan, Iza, Hela, Alina and a US marine.
'The soldiers were great . . . It was the first time I tried chewing gum.'

Boys at the Pahiatua Polish Children's Camp, 1945. Stefan, age 15, is kneeling, second from right, front row.

Pahiatua, 1945.
A photo taken at the Pahiatua camp shows Iza and Alina in matching striped pinafores made by their older sister, puff-sleeved white shirts with Peter Pan collars and oversized white bows in their hair . . . Completing the family trinity is Hela.

Helena (left, age 12) and Zofia (age 10) at the now-demolished grotto on the site of the Pahiatua Polish Children's Camp, 1974. *Between us is a piece of my father's past, slowly disappearing into history, just like his two little girls.*

i przyszli dni dliamnie skwaru, i potu
Łaska Boska nademno że dostaje
emeryturę z kolej dajo mi 800 złoty
miesęcznie tak że mi naryce wystarczy
tylko zdrowie moje marne i wszystko
mnie boli przewurne nogi bolo i do tego
oczy mi się psojo tak że i ukulary
mi niepomogojo

    tak że ja do Was kochane dzieci
jak jeszcze Bóg pozwol mi żyć to
chiba do Was pisae jusz nie będę mugł
bo oczy moje niewidzo, i dzierzawa
moja konczysię prędko

Pasyłamy ukłony i pozdrowienia dla
Chesia z żono i wnóczkien Kaziowi z żono
Stefanowi z żono Heli Hencowi oraz
najmlodrym Fze, i Alucky
Bądcie zdrowi i rostawajcie z Bogiem
Najwyzrym. Synaczkowie milojciesię ,,

Całoje i ścieska moa Ojcec

Ojcec prosi abyś
ak najpredzej
wysłał ten list
do Heli
Pozdrowienia do Lidii i do Basi~

Józef

do w. Lyszreng

Józef's letter to his children in New Zealand, circa 1961, possibly his last:
'Keep well. I'm leaving you in God's care. Your loving father, Józef.'

the children had arrived in 1944. The facility had been built early in the war on the site of the old Pahiatua racecourse, about three kilometres south of the rural Wairarapa town. Its first occupants had been foreign enemy nationals, civilian internees of German, Italian and Japanese extraction. The camp had been renamed and repurposed in time for the children's arrival, but its bald, military construction style was nonetheless alarming to the young, war-scarred Poles. It was hugely reassuring, Dad says, to discover the welcoming flowers, Polish names on camp signposts, and freshly made beds. 'We each had our own little cupboards by our beds,' he still marvels. 'I'd never had anything like that before.' The regular, generous meals that came from the camp kitchen convinced them, once and for all, they were guests in this country, not prisoners.

'New Zealand was a beautiful country, we had everything more or less, and all the hunger was behind us. But we hadn't known normality really, not for years. We all went a bit wild, let loose in the fields, the bush, the river around the camp.'

The Polish government-in-exile had initially provided some funding for the camp, but this soon came to an end. The New Zealand government took over and the Polish staff, with the children assigned chores to support them, created vegetable gardens and took over the running of the kitchen and laundries. In early 1945, the first group of girls left the camp to attend New Zealand schools, Hela among them. That year, when my father turned 16, he was transferred with six other boys to secondary school in Auckland. Sacred Heart College was his first real experience of New Zealand life, and it was a shock. The Polish boys were welcomed by their classmates as celebrities on their first day, but their poor English and their awkwardness soon isolated them. 'I couldn't communicate. I couldn't learn. Everything was so strange,' Dad says. He left within a year, as soon as a trade apprenticeship could be found for him.

The transition from child to worker, he says, was another trauma. The New Zealanders he met were well meaning and kind, but had no idea about the politics that had shaped his experience of war and now its aftermath. Stefan's radical opinions and moody behaviour frequently caused tension in the households he lived in during his apprenticeship. 'They thought we were just children anyway, that we didn't know what we were talking about.' In one household, he simply stayed in his room to avoid having to talk to anyone. 'They thought there was something wrong with me.' But by the time he was 20, and despite a series of failed attempts to get a foothold in various trades, he was a qualified fitter and turner. 'My English was better, and I decided the world was not just Auckland. So just like that, I left.' He travelled around the South Island, taking itinerant labouring jobs at various hydro-electricity projects, and at one stage 'borrowing' an English name from a New Zealand friend he had lost touch with. For a few years, he transformed himself—on paper at least—into Barry Sutton, not complicated and foreign Stefan Wiśniewski. ('Barry had been my friend, a guy I'd worked with once and he owed me ten pounds.')

At the same time, Stefan sought out his Polish contacts in every city he went to, partying and drinking with the boys who had shared his experience of exile. He met my mother, he said, at one of these parties.

∼

'I don't know why he married me,' Mum says.

'What do you mean?' I ask. 'What do you mean you don't know why?'

I am warm in the morning sun of my kitchen, on the phone to my mother. She sounds upbeat, even animated, for someone

177

who is wondering whether she's been married to the wrong man for 54 years.

'I mean with the Jewish thing, the Russian thing. I had no idea what all that meant to him when we got married. But he knew. He knew who I was.'

'Mum, I think he was in love with you. That's what he told me.'

'Ha. I don't know about that. But don't tell him about Gorky.'

More secrets. My mother loves subterfuge. Even at 79 years of age, she's not beyond playing games. 'Come on Mum, you have to tell him. He'll understand.'

'No he won't. He's not interested anyway.'

My mother has had another email from her nephew in Sydney, the son of one of her estranged half-brothers, John. I've never met Darian, and neither has she. We have been peering at Darian's postage stamp-sized photo online, trying to work out if it's his dark eyes, his lack of hair or his oval face that makes him look so eerily familiar, so much like the images of a middle-aged Joseph Zam, Mum's father. My half-cousin is a graphic artist and keen family genealogist and has clearly decided to ignore old family grudges and track my mother down.

'Don't be nervous,' Darian wrote in his first email to Mum last year. 'I had really given up getting a resolution to this.' Since then, the fractured family my mother gave up on years ago has been taking shape, on paper at least.

Yesterday, Darian sent Mum a photograph of Joseph that she had never seen before. In it, her father is a serious 10-year-old with prominent ears, posing with his mother Hannah and two younger sisters. We now have a photo of my Russian great-grandmother, the woman buried in Karori's Jewish cemetery, and whose image for me has until now been limited to that blank headstone. But Hannah is dour and thin-lipped in this photograph. Her dark, striped shirt, with a pocket watch pinned above her left breast, rises almost to her chin from a tightly-belted waist. Her arms arch protectively around her two daughters, who are enveloped by her long skirts. Joseph stands by her side, aloof, a book in his right hand, firmly closed. Hannah and her daughters, little girls in matching dresses, wear identical tear-shaped earrings, perhaps pearls, which hover below their earlobes. All dead, I think. All dead.

But Darian has more. The surprise is a short memoir written by another of Hannah's daughters, Liza, the sister who immigrated to New Zealand with my grandfather in 1916. When I ask Darian about the source of this material he explains it was Liza's grandson, another stranger to my mother, who gave 'all this new stuff' to him. 'It blows me away,' my cousin admits. The piece is clearly written with an audience in mind. It has a title, an author.

'My early life in Czarist Russia, by Liza Mann,' my great aunt begins.

I wonder about Liza's careful choice of the word 'Czarist'. She's not writing about any old Russia, that title seems to say, certainly not the bleak and much-maligned Russia of the Cold War era. Liza, then Mrs Jack Mann of Glen Road, Kelburn, would have been writing from her Wellington desk about a Russia already mothballed and consigned to history. 'I was born of Jewish parents in the year 1894, in the city of Feodosiya, Crimea, on the Black Sea, approximately 200 miles from the city of Yalta,' Liza says.

She describes her childhood years: her successful jeweller and watchmaker father ('he looked after all of the city's main buildings' clocks') and the society connections this work gave him that allowed her to attend school from the age of six ('I loved every minute of it . . . I was very thrilled because education was only for the rich and privileged'). Liza recalls, too, her parents' insistence that she take up an apprenticeship as a dressmaker; her wasted academic potential is clearly a grievance she nurses many years later. She is devastated when told by her father she must decline a scholarship to a prestigious secondary school. 'I asked him why in a very calm way . . . He told me your older sisters and brother had no proper schooling, only from a private teacher, and that the three younger members of the family would not have the chance given to me. He didn't want me to be ashamed of them.'

The fragility of Liza's world is clear; the difficulties of life as a young Jewish woman give way to a jolt from the pages of history. 'When I was about nine or 10 years old the battleship Potemkin and some other ships came to Feodosiya and tried to start a revolution against the Czar,' she writes. 'The army and police made us take all the food and bedding and everything we could carry such as wheelbarrows, wagons—anything that could carry us—and we went up into the hills and into the valley . . . The revolt did not last long as there was no cooperation with the navy by the military of the town or the police. The ships left for Odessa where they were all captured.' The Potemkin did arrive in Feodsiya on 5 July 1905, but it was to Constanta, on the coast of Romania, that the ship was to sail to the following day, not Odessa.

Then, like the ships she has just described, my great aunt's story suddenly changes direction.

One day on Sunday when one of my sisters and I were outside the house a dark figure approached us and asked us if this was the Zam residence . . . My father was expecting him and came outside to meet him saying come inside Maxim. Father introduced me, saying this is Maxim Gorky.

I stopped at this point and reread the paragraph.

'Do you know who Maxim Gorky is?' I asked Mum. 'Do you believe this?'

Mum's upset that I need to ask. 'Yes, of course, he's the Russian writer. I don't know if it's true though. Maybe.'

'I looked at him and he was wearing a big black coat and a drooping felt hat,' Liza's story continues.

> When he took off his coat he was wearing dark trousers and a black satin shirt which was embroidered in the front, and over his trousers a black leather belt. Over this he was also wearing large leather boots. After that we met him often as he used to come to the house and have coffee with my father. He drank very black coffee with much sugar. In time I found out that Maxim Gorky was his pen name. My father had several photographs of him with his real name signed on them. I brought some of them with me but over the years they have become lost or misplaced. I can still see Gorky's figure before me.
>
> The same period in my life allowed me to meet some of his friends such as Leo Tolstoy. His books and plays especially Anna Karenina gave me many hours of pleasure as I read them. He was an imposing figure with his greyish beard. I also met the poet Pushkin, whose poems were very witty and enjoyable.

I want to believe Liza's story, which ends abruptly at this point, but her claim to have met Pushkin is alarming. Pushkin was born at the end of the 18th century and died in 1837 in Moscow, almost 60 years before Liza was born. It throws her other accounts into doubt. It just seems too unlikely that the daughter of a small-town Jewish jeweller met Tolstoy, or that Maxim Gorky visited her house on the coast of the Black Sea. But why, I wonder, would Liza lie about these encounters, especially in such intricate detail? It's as if she is holding up the embroidery on Gorky's satin shirt, his love of sugar in his coffee, as evidence of her veracity. I was there, she is saying, it was him.

I ask Darian for his opinion, and he is also a little sceptical. Liza had written this account in New Zealand in the early 1980s, he thinks, when she was in her 90s. 'I'm wondering whether her state of mind was so good at the time,' he writes to me. 'A lot of it makes no sense.' He wonders whether Liza is referring to Pushkin's poetry, rather than the man himself, or perhaps another literary figure from the period. But meetings with Gorky and Tolstoy are possible, he believes. 'Tolstoy would have been very old, she would have met him just before he died. Her description matches his physical appearance. I transcribed her writing word for word; the English is broken in places. It was written out by her husband Jack, I think.'

At the turn of the century, the Zam family was living in a Russia on the cusp of transformation in a region alive with artistic and revolutionary energy. Gorky was already a well-known writer of short stories and plays; he was also a Marxist and an active member of the Social Democrat party. When he was arrested and then exiled from St Petersburg and Moscow in 1901 for political activities, Gorky did move to the Crimea, a popular Black Sea holiday destination for artists and intelligentsia. Anton Chekhov lived in nearby Yalta, and Leo Tolstoy, who was aged and ailing, resided at the town of Gaspra. Gorky, like Chekhov, suffered from tuberculosis; the Crimea's sunny dry climate and surrounding mountains made it a popular destination for those seeking a cure.

It's well documented that Gorky visited Chekhov in Yalta; Gorky also published accounts of his visits to Tolstoy at the elderly author's home in 1901 and 1902. 'These fragmentary notes,' Gorky writes in his introduction to *Reminiscences of Lev Nikolayevich Tolstoy*, 'were written by me during the period when I lived in Liese and Lev Nikolayevich [Tolstoy] at Gaspra in the Crimea. They cover the period of Tolstoy's serious illness and of his subsequent recovery. The notes were carelessly jotted down on scraps of paper, and I thought I had lost them, but recently I have found some of them . . .' Photographs of the two men from those Crimean years show them just as Liza describes: Gorky, who would have been in his 30s, in his black shirt, leans on an ornate porch post in 1902. Tolstoy, in his 70s, with his trailing white beard, is seated in the garden at Gaspra in a photograph taken by his daughter. A 1953 Soviet painting by Alexey Ignatyevich Kirillov, *Maxim Gorky visiting Leo Tolstoy in Gaspra in 1902,* depicts the two men together, talking on a sun-dappled balcony, Tolstoy seated in a wicker chair, Gorky standing tall in knee-high black boots, the blue horizon of the Black Sea beyond him.

What, though, would bring Maxim Gorky to Feodosiya, to the Zam house? Gorky was an artist; he was also a revolutionary. Unlike Tolstoy, he had an underprivileged and unhappy peasant childhood (Gorky was a pen name chosen for its meaning: 'bitter') and he'd travelled Russia on foot as a vagrant youth, an experience he was fond of calling his 'university'. He was also an outspoken opponent of the anti-Semitism that pervaded Russian society at the time, a violent bigotry endorsed by the Czarist regime. Maybe Aaron, Liza's Jewish father, my Jewish great-grandfather, was Marxist too. Many Jews were. Maybe Gorky visited the Zam household in Feodosiya, where my grandfather would have been an impressionable 10-year-old, for political meetings. I suggest it to my mother.

'I suppose that might explain my father's tattoo,' she says.

Mum has told me about the hammer-and-sickle tattoo, the symbol of Soviet socialism, that Joseph wore on his forearm. It was just another thing he had always refused to discuss with her. And it had been—as far as I know, still is—another shameful secret my mother has kept from her husband, my communist-phobic father. It's no consolation to Mum that her businessman father might have regretted his youthful hammer-and-sickle tattoo and was perhaps too ashamed to talk about it in later life. It doesn't help either when I tell her that Gorky died in 1936, before World War II, and in mysterious circumstances; it's rumoured that he was murdered on Stalin's orders. My mother knows only that Gorky was a poster boy for Stalin's socialist regime, the same regime that sent her husband and his Polish family into exile and many millions of others to their deaths. Gorky's potential link to her Jewish family, the fact that her grandmother may have served him coffee in her Crimean home, is something she cannot bring herself to discuss with my father. He would never understand, she says.

'See, I don't know why he married me,' Mum says. 'I don't know why.'

After we say goodbye, her words are ringing in my ears. From my warm spot in the sun in the kitchen, the phone silent in my hand, my mother's dilemma suddenly becomes clear. All the history of Europe, its centuries of hatreds and grievances, an unshakeable and terrible legacy, has found a new stage. This time it's playing out far from the continent that gave rise to it, oceans away and generations later, in my elderly parents' living room.

9

memory's bell repeats its great terror
memory's bell beats an unceasing alarm

Zbigniew Herbert, 'From an Unwritten Theory of Dreams'

In the early 1980s, when I was still single and working in Wellington, I had a phone call from my mother.

'Your father's in hospital,' she'd said. 'They don't know what it is, some sort of viral thing, but he's pretty miserable. Don't worry though; I'm sure he'll be fine. I just thought you should know.'

I was alarmed; my father was never sick, certainly never sick enough for hospital. This was more than a daughter's naive view of her untouchable and larger-than-life parent. He'd always had a wiry strength that set him apart. If he had survived deportation to Siberia, surely he was impervious to the hazards that diminished softer, less tested middle-aged men? But I sensed my mother was as rattled as I was; maybe that's why I went home.

I wasn't prepared for the sight of his weakened and miserable frame in a hospital bed. The multi-storey block of Whakatane hospital had floated ominously above our low-rise streets throughout my childhood, but I had never been inside before. Now, from the doorway of that fourth floor room, I saw both my father and my hometown in a new and unnerving light. His normally robust body seemed bony under the white sheets, his olive face greyed and diminished. Beyond the bed, through the

185

dust-splattered window behind him, the enormous blue haze of the Pacific Ocean dwarfed the lumpy outline of Whale Island and the grid-like streets below.

'You look mysterious,' he said to me, waving at the mask they had made me put on before I could come in. If he's trying to be funny, I thought, he must be okay.

'You look a bit peaky,' I replied. 'How are you feeling?'

'Not good, to tell you the truth. Not good at all. You know, Helena, I think this might be the end for me.'

I choked. 'Come on Dad, this isn't the end for you. This is just some sort of infection.'

'No, they don't know what it is. They have no idea. It could be anything. But you know, we all have to go some time.'

When I asked Mum what had happened, she said he'd lost his appetite and had put himself to bed. For several days in a row, she'd arrived home from work to find him still a huddle under the bedclothes. 'He never does that. He never stays in bed. So I made him go to the doctor. Then he rang me from the hospital.' Dad was correct: the doctors couldn't pinpoint the cause of his sudden illness. After three days they sent him home, but not before he'd read a *Reader's Digest* in the ward's waiting room that changed his life, he told me later. It featured an article in which the author claimed that regular walking had helped him make a full and miraculous recovery from a life-threatening illness. Dad couldn't remember what the author's illness was. 'But I'm going to try it, the walking,' he said when I rang from Wellington a few days later. 'It can't make me feel any worse.'

He began with 10-minute strolls that left him weak and shaky but within a year he was walking for hours every day. When he took early retirement from the paper mill and shift work in 1989, the walks lengthened. He explored the bushy coastal tracks between Whakatane and its neighbouring beach, Ohope, and then began making his own paths, illegally following cattle trails across farmland and through privately owned pine forests. He'd carry a backpack in the summer months to collect firewood for their winter log burner, or a plastic bag for mushrooms in autumn. His expeditions also broadened in scope, sometimes reaching as far afield as Mt Ruapehu, where he'd leave the car parked outside the Department of Conservation headquarters at Whakapapa and circumnavigate the mountain's lower slopes alone. He'd stay in mountain huts next to young German tourists (his least favourite kind, he'd tell us bluntly, as they were so noisy and thoughtless), living off canned sardines, water crackers and his new favourite food, two-minute noodles. 'Your father's gone again,' Mum would say when I rang. 'He says he'll be back on Tuesday.' We laughed at his evangelical faith in the benefits of walking but also admired it. He was fit and, as he aged, healthier than most of his peers. He'd also, we noticed belatedly, almost stopped drinking.

I ask him now about the mysterious illness and his spell in hospital and he only just remembers it. He certainly doesn't remember telling me he was dying. 'I just remember feeling so weak,' he says, 'like I did when I was in Uzbekistan. I couldn't move.

'You know, maybe it was the same thing that I had then, some sort of recurrence. Or maybe it was something else. Maybe I was depressed.'

~

In 1998, with a desperation that I can't fathom 15 years later, I wanted to get pregnant. Tolerant and level-headed James tried to put my obsession into perspective. Our five-year-old daughter, Anna—blond, tough and oblivious to my concerns—would be fine without a younger sibling. She wouldn't be ruined, or spoilt, or even lonely. Life would just be a little bit quieter, for all of us, he said. But I wasn't convinced.

'It's not the same for him,' I complained to my mother on the phone. 'He doesn't understand what it's like. I feel like time's running out. I can't sleep; it's doing my head in. And don't tell me to relax, because that's what I'm getting from everyone else.'

Mum sympathised and changed the subject.

'Your father's not sleeping either. He's wound up about the deck. It's still not finished.'

The wooden deck outside the living room of their little Lockwood house in Whakatane was the sunny spot most of their retirement hours were spent on. It offered an outlook over their neat, blunt-edged garden, and a white plastic table and chairs to view it from. My father wasn't a true gardener, approaching the aesthetics of their small garden the way a barber approached a head of hair: it was something to be kept under control. He was happy to nurture the tomato plants he bought each summer and the citrus and avocado trees that provided regular and useful harvests, some of which were delivered to my sister and me in plastic shopping bags on visits to Wellington. But the deep red rose that grew on a trellis and the camellias across the lawn had been inherited from the house's previous owner. They were subject to harsher treatment, and pruned liberally and viciously at regular intervals. My father credited every bloom that appeared to his 'tough love' gardening style, a miracle to be enjoyed and boasted about from their vantage point on the deck. But now some of the boards on the deck had rotted away and Dad was trying to rebuild it.

I remembered the collapsed chimney in our old house and the years it had taken for my father to complete that job. That hadn't worried him then.

'Why did you let him start doing it?' I asked my mother. 'He'll take forever. Can't you talk him into paying a builder?'

'No, there's something else going on. I don't think it's just the deck.'

A week later, Mum called again. This time, she said, the doctor had made a diagnosis: he was depressed. I remember being startled by the news, the reality of my father's mental health. Maybe my father wasn't as tough as I thought. Then, lost in my own melodrama, I became rudely unsympathetic. Dad had been prescribed anti-depressants, but had refused to speak to a counsellor.

'Why not?' I demanded. 'Why not take any help on offer?'

'Because he says there's nothing a counsellor could tell him that would make any difference,' Mum told me. 'What would a stranger know about his life?'

~

I wish I could say now I'd been a better daughter. I wish I could say I had visited more, had been a little more tolerant of my father's subdued voice on the phone, that I'd understood his muted and low-key congratulations months later when I told him I was finally, joyously, pregnant. My mother, instead, was his only support and sounding board. Whatever my father went through then, he went through without me. And he managed it the way he did in Uzbekistan, I realise now, with a simple force of will.

'It was the worst thing that happened to me, that depression,' he tells me. 'It was much worse than anything that happened in the war, much worse. I never want to go there again.'

Much worse than anything that happened in the war. Was this possible? It made me think about the night his sister, Hela, came to our door when I was a child, unexpected, like a stray animal. This was tricky territory; I realised we'd never talked about it before. When I asked him about it, Dad was thrown by the sudden shift in conversation. 'She wasn't well,' he said. 'Don't you remember?'

'Not really, no,' I answered.

In fact, I could remember some of it: the mist of shock in the house and Hela's O-shaped eyes and V-shaped cheekbones, glimpsed over my mother's shoulder in the dim light of the glassy porch. There must have been other things—smiles, tears, conversation or explanation—but those details had slipped away, like lights receding in a spooky fog.

I did understand then, somehow, that she had come on foot. The act of her walking astounded me. She'd put on her shoes and walked past the letterbox at the end of her Auckland driveway. She'd turned left at the footpath, south, away from her starched-linen house with the sad singsong marble clock on the mantelpiece and her husband in the blue armchair in the corner. I knew how long it took to drive that distance— windows down, singing 'You Are My Sunshine', stopping for lunch in Matamata—so what was in our little house almost 300 kilometres away that she needed so badly? Sanctuary? Did she have something to deliver, a note or a gift, in her pocket?

Dad told me that Hela had arrived at the Board Mills, on the outskirts of town, while he was at work. He'd had a message from the office that his sister was there for him; could he please take her somewhere. Hela was filthy and had clearly been sleeping on the side of the road. 'Oh my God, she smelt. It was terrible,' he said. 'I took her home and we ran a bath for her.' Then he rang Henek and booked a bus ticket for her back to Auckland the following day. I asked him why he was so quick to send her back. Maybe her arrival was a cry for help? Maybe she was fleeing Henek? No, he said, surprised that I should think that. Henek was a strange man, but he was a good and loyal husband. Henek just couldn't manage her when things got really bad.

'So why did she come to us? Why walk like that, all that way?'

'I don't know why she came,' he said. 'I have no idea. I think she just wanted to see me.'

~

In 2004, Dad was among those asked to contribute to *New Zealand's First Refugees: Pahiatua's Polish Children*, a book to celebrate the 60th anniversary of the children's arrival. Compiled by the Polish Children's Reunion Committee in Wellington, the book would contain recollections from the now elderly Poles, their own children, and others who had contact with them. But my father didn't take up the invitation.

'I can't write,' he said. 'I don't know what to say.'

I later bought a copy and read the Poles' stories of deportation, forced-labour camps, refuge in Iran, and life in post-war New Zealand. Every account seemed to carry the same mix of regret and thankfulness that had become so familiar to me. But near the end of the book was a short piece, less than a page long, loftily titled 'A Great Impression on My Life'. It was written by someone called Geoff Bennett. Bennett had been a teenager in New Plymouth shortly after the war, when his local Scout group took some of the Polish boys as billets for the holidays.

'The lad who stayed with us was Stefan Wiśniewski,' Geoff Bennett wrote, 'who was a splendid boy and as I remember was the saddest person I had ever met. He had a reason, of course.'

It was a shock to come across my father in the book's pages; I'd never heard about the New Plymouth holiday before and Geoff Bennett's name meant nothing to me. But Dad was thrilled. He remembered that holiday clearly, he told me, as if it were yesterday. He'd never kept in touch with the family who had been so kind to him. He didn't know why. The author's words, though, haunted me. I thought back to the younger, volatile father of my childhood, compared him with the mellow man who was now a gentle grandfather to my own children. Then it hit me. He was my father. How could I have missed the sadness?

Whenever I read the accounts of holocaust survivors, war veterans, and displaced and dislocated people, I found something eerily familiar in their stories. As a child, I read and reread Anne Frank's *Diary of a Young Girl,* amazed by her naive and terrible optimism: 'I feel the suffering of millions. And yet, when I look up at the sky, I somehow feel that everything will change for the better, that this cruelty too will end.' It didn't change for the better; she *died,* I wanted to scream. They *killed* her. When the unbearably brave Kyrstyna also died on the Gobi Desert trek in Slawomir Rawicz's *The Long Walk*—another horrifyingly true story with echoes of my father's journey—I cried for the first time ever onto a book's pages. The resilience of the children in Ian Serraillier's *The Silver Sword* both repelled and fascinated me: how did they manage it? Was I trying to work it out even then? These were more than stories. I knew these things happened because they had happened to my father. Children could say their prayers, help their parents, do well at school, and *still* suffer. All it took was a knock on the door in the night.

So this was my father's monstrous legacy: a childhood trauma that he was lucky to survive and that cast a long shadow over mine. But I needed to see him through a stranger's eyes to recognise the damage. The impact of my young father's grief on Geoff Bennett, so accurately and casually diagnosed many years after a fleeting childhood interaction, was terrifyingly clear. It was the grief of exile that Vladimir Nabokov wrote so exquisitely of: not a sorrow for lost banknotes, but for the longed-for homecoming that would never take place, 'a hypertrophied sense of lost childhood'. My father had carried that sadness throughout his adult life like Hela's ugly sack of onions, a burden he couldn't put down, even if he wanted to. I couldn't measure it or compare it with traumas, private or public, others had suffered. Was it bigger, or lumpier, than the load carried by any victim of violence, disaster, genetic bad luck or family breakdown? Was it any worse than the grief felt by my abandoned mother? But perhaps the scale of the misery was irrelevant. It was there. It was simply 'one of the great laws of the human soul', as DH Lawrence wrote: '. . . a bruise which only slowly deepens its terrible ache, till it fills all the psyche. And when we think we have recovered and forgotten, it is then that the terrible after-effects have to be encountered at their worst.'

And once I'd recognised it, this understanding was everywhere, following me, tapping me on the shoulder like a ghost. I couldn't ignore it any more. My childhood wish for my father's happy-ever-after ending in New Zealand was never going to come true. I wasn't the daughter of a hero; I was the daughter of a damaged survivor.

~

In the family's early years in New Zealand, Hela gave every impression she had put the war behind her. She took her role as family caregiver seriously; she was capable, strong, and deeply religious. She was not only a fine needleworker but a skilled and prolific seamstress. In Iran, where many of the older girls had taken classes in sewing, Hela had made intricate and colourful Polish costumes for her little sisters. In New Zealand, she made all of their clothes.

A photo taken at the Pahiatua camp shows Iza and Alina in matching striped pinafores made by their older sister, puff-sleeved white shirts with Peter Pan collars, and oversized white bows in their hair. Their ankle socks are only just visible in the overgrown country grass at their feet and the Tararuas are a grey outline on the horizon. Completing the family trinity is Hela. She stands behind her little sisters wearing a dark, tailored blazer, protective hands resting on their shoulders. Her hair is lifting from her neck in the Wairarapa wind.

What was it that drove my serious young aunt? Her siblings remember her as strong but, like all of them, extremely homesick. By the time this photo was taken, Hela would have known that a return to Poland was impossible. It seemed her future, their future, was to be played out in New Zealand. But little about this country could have felt right. For all the children, the experience of deportation had produced a suspicion of strangers, of their potential to be hostile, even dangerous. Security lay in the familiar, and Hela had already turned to her fellow Poles and to her faith in an attempt to find a foothold in New Zealand. As one of the older orphans, she had been among the first to leave the Polish shelter of the Pahiatua camp. Her first stop had been Wellington, where she'd been a student at the Convent of the Sacred Heart, later Erskine College, in Island Bay. Then she'd moved to Auckland to train as a nurse with the Sisters of Mercy at Mater Hospital in Epsom. This was a religious calling, Iza believes, not a career.

'She loved it with the Sisters,' Iza says. 'If things had worked out, she would have become a nun. She really wanted be a nun. She would have been very happy with that life. But she had to look after us; she'd promised Mum.'

When she was still in Wellington, Hela made regular weekend trips to the Pahiatua camp to visit Kazik and her younger sisters. Both Iza and Alina remember the dread they felt at her arrival and the intensity of their older sister's expectations that they should dress neatly and behave properly.

'I didn't think about my big sister until she came to see us,' Iza says. 'When she was with us, Hela was very domineering. She definitely thought of herself as our guardian. I was happy when she left and we could relax again with the other children.'

The camp was to remain home for the younger girls for a

number of years. 'I liked my life at Pahiatua,' Iza says. 'I was happy.' After the misery of their early childhood, my young aunts were adjusting. Life centred not on the new country that had offered them shelter, or even on their older siblings, but on the bonds they were making with the other orphans. Outside the daily camp routines of Polish lessons, religious rituals and meals, the children were happy to run wild in the local countryside. They avoided when they could the sometimes unpredictable and moody adult staff in charge. But when it became clear the camp would close, Hela lobbied hard with the Catholic authorities to make sure Kazik and her sisters could attend schools in Auckland. First Iza, in 1948, and then Alina, in 1949, were allotted sought-after charity places at Sacred Heart School, now Baradene, in Auckland. Kazik, too, after a short time in the Polish Boys' Hostel that was set up in Hawera, went to Auckland's Sacred Heart College. Hela was determined what was left of the little family unit would stay intact and near her. Iza and Alina remember Hela's first home in Auckland, a house owned by a piano teacher in Mt Eden. The girls would stay with her on their weekends away from boarding school: long and dull days spent quietly with their serious older sister. But school was no better.

'I hated that school,' Iza says. 'I was so homesick for my friends from the camp.'

Iza and Alina were still struggling with English and increasingly relied on each other for support. The two other Polish girls at the school were daygirls: they were lucky, Iza says, because they had mothers and homes to return to at night. My aunts, who were boarding, were isolated. 'The teachers, the other girls, they never let us forget we were charity girls, that we should be grateful,' Iza says. 'It was awful. When I failed School Certificate, Hela was so ashamed of me, so disappointed. If there was a bridge, I swear I would have jumped off it. I made a promise to myself then that I would never, never, be a failure at something again.'

Then the sisters were told that Hela was marrying.

'We found out he was a Polish army officer she'd been writing to,' Iza says. 'They were setting up a house in Auckland. She was getting married to give us a home. She married Henek because of us.'

~

Hela was my godmother; she must have been at my baptism. But I can't find a photo of the two of us, the two Helenas, together. In fact there isn't a photo anywhere of the event: it's as if it never happened. Even my parents look at each other and shrug when I ask for details.

'I know we had your baptism in Whakatane,' Mum says, 'but I can't remember much any more.'

Dad nods. 'Family came, the family was there,' he says.

'What family? Who?'

'It's terrible, I don't know who any more,' Dad says. 'Sorry. I don't know. It's all gone. But Hela was there. Yes, she must have been there.'

In 1962, the year I was born, my aunt would have been 38 years old. She had been married to Henek Torbus, who was almost 50, for 10 years. The couple had a small house in Papatoetoe, no children and—it must have been clear even then—little in common other than their shared heritage. They had been married in Auckland after a short courtship conducted through an exchange of letters. My father, then in his early 20s, doesn't remember much of their wedding day and nothing at all of the wedding Mass or the church in which it was held. 'I know they had the reception in Mt Eden,' he says. 'That's all I remember.' But he does recall being unimpressed by his sister's husband, whose receding hairline and serious manner made him seem even older than he was.

'He wasn't my type,' Dad says. 'He was very regimented, very different from me. I was still all over the place, still very young.'

Henek was a decorated Polish army officer who had served with allied forces in North Africa. His *Virtuti Militari*, the Polish equivalent of the Victoria Cross, had been awarded for bravery at the 1941 siege of Tobruk in Libya, where he'd charged and captured a German machine-gun post. But at the end of the war he was effectively homeless. Like many of the Poles who had fought with the Allies against Germany, Henek chose permanent exile rather than return to a Poland under Russian communist control. In 1947, after two years in United Kingdom resettlement camps, he was offered assisted passage to Tasmania. Several hundred Polish soldiers, members of the Polish Carpathian Rifle Brigade who had fought with the Australian 'Rats of Tobruk' in the defence of the Libyan port, were offered work on hydroelectric schemes and other public works in Tasmania's isolated central highlands. Many of the Polish men turned up on the first day of employment still dressed in their military uniforms, the only clothes they possessed. Then, towards the end of his two-year contract, Henek placed an ad in the newsletter of Auckland's newly formed Polish Association, looking for a female penpal. Hela answered.

Why would Hela, who had wanted so much to be a nun, and who had never shown any interest in men, marry someone more than 10 years older, someone she barely knew? Like Iza, Dad hasn't any doubts about Hela's motivations: his sister was looking for security. She wanted to create a home for herself and, perhaps more importantly, the siblings she had promised to look after. And Henek's pedigree was, at least by pre-war Polish standards, impeccable. In the traditional and class-conscious society she had known, my aunt's new husband would have been a hero, a man who would have given her significant social standing. Perhaps Hela didn't understand—or maybe she didn't care—that in her new reality, in post-war New Zealand, Henek's military honours and pretensions were meaningless. To his Kiwi work colleagues and neighbours, my uncle would have been just another unskilled foreign labourer with a strange name, isolated by his poor English and lack of desire to assimilate. Her decision to marry him was characteristically noble, but misjudged.

'It wasn't love,' Dad says to me now, sadly. 'I know it wasn't about love.'

I wonder what Hela felt on the day she married a man she barely knew, the day my father cannot recall. I think back to my own wedding day, to my total absence of fear. I remember James reaching for my hand when we stood in the church, and the overwhelming reassurance of his grip. I remember emerging with him from the building before anyone else—just for a few seconds, alone—into the Saturday afternoon sun and standing under the swaying macrocarpas outside. And I remember Hela's pale and smiling face under a crocheted hat.

~

The wedding gift Hela gave us that day in 1991—the only memento I now have of my aunt—was a linen tablecloth, the kind of cloth few people use any more. It was fringed in intricate silk crochet and embroidered with russet poppies, each tiny, perfect stitch made by hand.

I don't remember receiving the tablecloth and, as my wedding day fades to a blur, I don't remember much of my elderly aunt's presence. The photos, though, show Hela with her face typically free of make-up, her husband beside her in his ill-fitting suit. In that smart crowd of young professionals and their middle-aged counterparts, my uncle and aunt would have been, as usual, out of place. I was aware of Hela only once, when my father made a speech to the already tipsy crowd at the early evening dinner.

Dad, I knew, was terrified. He wasn't a public speaker. His speech notes were carefully written on a piece of paper, folded and refolded into a tight and furry bundle that he had placed in the top pocket of his rented morning suit. As he stood, and the room's clatter quietened at the cue of a tinkled glass, I waited for him to reach into the pocket and unfold the piece of paper. But he didn't. He'd already started speaking—'Hello everyone,' he said, smiling, nervous—when I realised he was too paralysed by nerves to move his hand to his pocket. My heart began to thump. So this is when my wedding goes wrong, I thought. I listened as he pushed painfully on, my hand clammy against the cold glass of champagne as he struggled. I tried to smile, concentrating on the bubbles, tracing the lines of their upward trajectory through the condensation with a finger. *Get your notes out of your pocket. Breathe. Hurry up.*

'Helena,' my father was saying, so slowly it seemed he was thinking about each syllable as it left his mouth, searching in the chaos of his thoughts for the next, 'you have been . . . a wonderful daughter.'

I scanned the now near-silent crowd in front of me. In that darkening room of people, my eyes fell on Hela. My aunt was no more distinct than anyone else, but to me she seemed to sit at its very centre, her eyes fixed on her brother. Her face was glistening in the summer heat as he spoke, her crochet hat tipped back on her pale forehead. She sat back from the table with her hands tucked on her lap, the food on the plate in front of her untouched. It was as if each of Dad's halting words could be for her, the other Helena in that room, as much as for me. She was entranced and not in the least worried by her brother's performance. When my father finally lifted his glass from the table in front of him and proposed a toast—'to the bride and groom', looking for the first time at me, the relief in his voice clear—Hela stood, clapping, grinning.

On the drive home to Auckland the following day, from the back seat of Iza and Mietek's car, Hela announced that it had been a 'fairy-tale' wedding. I hope now she was pleased she had come. Perhaps our wedding, with its curious blend of Kiwi and Polish traditions—the morning suits, the vodka shots, the hats—was evidence, if she needed it, that the future of her family in New Zealand was no longer in any doubt. This country wasn't the traditional utopia my Eastern European grandparents would have wanted for their family. That utopia, a world centred on faith, nationhood and family, had been washed away by history, along with the stigma of dislocation and displacement in this one. My sister and I had never been strangers in New Zealand and our children would never consider that they might be. I hope now that Hela understood this was the pay-off for the suffering she'd experienced in her lifetime. I doubt whether anyone thanked her. I know I didn't. My wedding day was the last time I saw her.

Today Hela's tablecloth is stored in a cardboard box, a relic at the bottom of my linen cupboard. I don't think I've ever used it on a table, but I take it out sometimes to admire. It's an extraordinary example of her legendary skill and determination. The glossy, tightly stitched flowers and feathery sheaves of wheat sit on a rough weave of natural linen, the pattern as flawless on the reverse as it is right side up. And it smells, I swear, of Hela's Palmolive house and the little sunroom by the kitchen where she kept her unfinished stitching under the hinged lid of the window seat. I can still hold the cloth to my face and inhale my past.

10

For all its charms, the island is uninhabited,
and the faint footprints scattered on its beaches
turn without exception to the sea.

As if all you can ever do here is leave
and plunge, never to return, into the depths.
Into unfathomable life.

Wisława Szymborska, 'Utopia'

The windscreen wipers slap a rhythm as we drive past the Botanic Garden, his favourite walking place, and blossoms whip across the wet road like spinning confetti. My father stares at the garden's familiar paths as we drive past.

'Do you think those girls understood that I wasn't frightened in Siberia?' he says now. 'I wanted to say that, but I don't think I did.'

He's talking about the classroom of 11-year-old girls he spoke to this morning. I know he would have preferred to be out walking, despite the weather. He gave the talk as a favour for me. A friend had asked if he'd speak to her daughter's class and I'd assured her he would be happy to. But when we'd arrived at the school this morning, Dad had been subdued. He hoped the girls had questions, he told me, because he hadn't prepared anything.

'So lovely for them to hear from someone who was actually there,' the blond teacher had said over her shoulder as we'd followed her through the school's crowded corridors into the classroom. The girls were studying the Polish children's journey and were writing fictional diaries; she hoped Dad's first-person story would add colour to their accounts. Her eyes had flicked to the watch on her wrist. 'It makes it so much more real, having you here. And it's wonderful that you've brought some slides,' she said, looking at me. Inside the empty classroom, she offered my father a chair. He declined and remained standing, hands in his pockets, watching as the girls began to arrive, filling the desks and tables. Then the lights dimmed and the screen at the front of the room filled with a black-and-white image of my grandparents.

'This is Mr Wiśniewski,' the teacher said. 'He's going to talk to us about his journey to New Zealand through Siberia.' The girls were silent, their faces pale in the reflected light of the white screen. The teacher looked to Dad, who remained quiet, standing.

'So, maybe to get us started, you could tell us about where you lived, Stefan, when you were small,' she prompted.

'Well, it was a small house. We had no electricity, no running water, no bathroom.'

'And what about bedrooms?'

'Well, no. We had no bedrooms. None. We all slept together, on the floor.' I watched some of the girls glance at each other and begin taking notes. 'We didn't have much money,' Dad was explaining. 'And there were 11 children.'

As the minutes passed, I saw my father relax just a little; he became absorbed in his own story. He was patient with the girls' sometimes off-track questions and their focus on the horrors of the experience. Yes, he told them, some children did get left behind at railway stations; yes, he did eat grass, he was hungry. But the bell in the hall rang before he was finished and the girls left the classroom as abruptly as they had arrived. Not to worry, the teacher said as she walked us to the school foyer, it's a big story.

Now that it's all over, he's relieved and upbeat. I've forgotten how nervous he gets in the spotlight. I remember the man who stood at the front of my classroom almost 40 years earlier to share that same past with a room of cynical teenagers, one of them his daughter. Had he been nervous then? Had he been dreading that school event just as much as I had? It had never occurred to me at the time that he might be; I remember only how miserable his presence made me feel. Now that I know my father doesn't like public speaking, that he never has, I feel sorry that I pushed him into today's presentation.

'You did a really good job, Dad. I think the girls enjoyed it.'

'Well, when I talk about it like that it's hard to believe it happened at all,' he says. 'I sometimes can't believe it myself.' There's a short silence in the car, and he turns his head to the gardens again. 'Do you think it's an accident, that I ended up here in New Zealand? That I didn't end up somewhere else? Or dead?'

When I don't respond immediately to his question, he continues. 'I just mean, it all seems so strange, don't you think, that it should be an accident?'

'I don't know Dad, I really don't,' I say. 'I know your sisters think it was God's will, that it was part of a bigger plan that you all made it here.'

'Well, I don't deny it. I prayed all the time during the war. When I was safe in Persia, and my mother was still in Russia with Hela, when we didn't know what had happened to them, I prayed so hard for them to be safe. I was just a kid and I prayed. And my prayers were answered. So you tell me, is this just a lucky thing? Or is it something else?'

'I'm sorry Dad, I just don't know.'

I do know what my father would like me to say. But the legacy he has probably hoped for, the deep religious faith he tried so hard to instil in us as children, with the rituals of Sunday Mass and singsong bedside prayer, has failed to take hold.

'Is it bad,' my 14-year-old son, Jeremy, asked me the other day, 'that I don't believe in God? Do you mind?'

Yes, I do mind, I wanted to say. You're too young to be so cynical and your grandfather would be heartbroken if he knew. My mind had flicked then to the religious picture that had hung above my sister's bed when we were children, a pastel-coloured image of a blond, kneeling boy overshadowed by a white-robed and feather-winged guardian angel. The angel's arms were uplifted in benediction; his eyes were gracefully lowered towards his charge. I remembered how comforting I had found that image when I was small. How could I explain that to my teenage son? Instead, I told Jeremy not to give up on God just yet and resolved not to mention his announcement to my father.

It's my responsibility, I know, that my son doesn't believe—that none of my children do. I've never talked to them about the faith that was such a big part of my childhood. Neither Zofia nor I attend Mass anymore. Our children are baptised, but are strangers to Catholicism. It was never a conscious decision, this drift away from belief, but it would now take more than my father's nudging to prompt a return. Faith is a topic we rarely discuss. It's a little like my mother's Jewishness; there's nothing to be gained from exposing the issue to family scrutiny. Outwardly, Dad seems resigned to his daughters' lapsed faith and to our secular Kiwi children. But I know he prays for our souls. He always has.

~

I've never been to the church in Berhampore, St Joachim's, before. It's disappointingly plain: a mid-century red brick rectangle, sandwiched between small wooden houses and pine trees at the end of a cul-de-sac. From the outside, there's nothing to distinguish it as the spiritual home of this city's Polish community. I think of the white dome that sets the local Greek Orthodox Church apart, and the pillars and spires of the Indian community's cultural centre only a few kilometres away. Inside St Joachim's, 30 white-haired people, most of them strangers to me, fill the back two pews on each side of the aisle.

I follow my father and my cousin Alicja to one of those two rows. An elderly couple shuffle sideways on the pew to make room for us, Polish missals on their laps. She wears a camel-coloured winter coat buttoned to her neck, and her lips are moving as she prays, silently. She doesn't look at us, but her husband lifts one hand in silent greeting and smiles at my father. I sit with Alicja, while Dad drops to his knees next to me, makes the sign of the cross and closes his eyes. On an outside aisle, sitting a little apart from the others, I can see my friend Marysia's parents. Her mother is still tall, but now stooped and greyed; she is seated and staring at the rows of empty pews before her. Her father is kneeling, like my father, with his head bowed. I wonder if I should talk to them later, ask how they are getting on at the rest home next door, but I decide against it. They won't remember me. Beyond them, at the front of the church, carpeted stairs lead to an empty wooden altar. A Madonna and child painting retrieved from the chapel altar at the Pahiatua camp hangs behind it, next to a drooping Polish flag.

'Why doesn't anyone sit at the front?' I whisper to Dad when he sits up.

'I don't know,' he says. 'They never do. They like it back here.'

It had been his idea that we'd come to Polish Mass. Alicja was visiting for the weekend, and she was keen to go, he said. What else was I doing on Sunday morning?

'I won't be able to understand what's going on,' I'd said. 'Or sing.'

'That's okay. I'll sing for you, no problem.' He wasn't deterred by my reluctance. I would be going with them.

I have to admit I'm curious; I want to meet these new friends of my father's. Dad has been a regular attendee at this weekly Mass since his arrival in Wellington two years ago. The elderly Poles who make up the bulk of the congregation didn't recognise him when he first started turning up, this man with a familiar name who had lived outside their close circle for so many years. Now he goes with them to the nearby cinema for coffee afterwards. And it's been a while since I went to Mass. In some ways, I miss the quiet ritual that used to define my Sundays. I think we all do, even my non-Catholic mother. Over the years, Mum seems to have adopted Catholicism by default, informally, almost by osmosis, in much the same way as she has adopted Polish food. When we were children, she would take us to Mass when Dad was on shift work and, until we became teenagers and less enthusiastic, would happily drop us at choir practice. After my sister and I left home, she would sometimes accompany Dad on Sundays. It was easy in Whakatane; she knew the church and could recognise some of the local faces. Here in Wellington, though, it's a double exclusion: she's not Catholic, nor is she one of them. The proceedings are conducted entirely in Polish, both inside and outside.

'There's no point,' she tells me. 'It's his thing.'

Today, as I feared, Mass is long, the sermon unintelligible. The priest seems miles away from us, fussing about at a distant altar. Around me, Polish voices chant responses to his prayers in a rhythm that I can't grasp. Alicja seems to have more of an idea about what's going on; she knows some of the Polish responses, can say some of the prayers. I follow their 'sit down', 'kneel', and 'stand up' prompts, my mouth stubbornly shut. At the final hymn, also unfamiliar to me, the unaccompanied voices around me are surprisingly vehement. My father sings loudly, as promised, to make up for my silence.

'This is my daughter, Helena, and my niece, Alicja,' he says to a circle of men in the sunshine outside. 'They thought they would come and see what we get up to here.' They all laugh, offer their hands, and glance at my father, my cousin and then at me, as if checking for authenticity.

'Hey,' one of the men says to Alicja and me, putting his hand on my shoulder. 'I've got a joke for you both.' He's grinning, excited, and I glimpse, just for a moment, the blue-eyed boy who would have stared through finger-marked train windows at his new Kiwi home in 1944. Now he must be close to 80 years old, wearing a zip-up jacket over a polo shirt that he's tucked into his belted slacks.

'What hurts more,' he says, 'a woman giving birth to a baby or a man getting kicked in the balls?'

I look at my father, who's grinning now too. I don't know whether we are being made fun of; we are less than five minutes out of church.

'I don't know,' I say. 'Do I have to guess?'

'Yep,' the man says.

'Childbirth?'

'No, you are wrong, sorry. A woman, she has one baby and then, surprise, she decides she wants to have another. A man, he gets kicked in the balls and he never, never wants to get kicked in the balls again. So this must hurt worse.'

The man roars with laughter, as does my father. I have no idea what has just happened. I'm reminded of the awkward evening spent in Kashan with Second Ali, where Alicja and I were the veiled bystanders in what proved to be another masculine dialogue.

'He's always like that,' Dad says later, on our way home in the car. 'He's very funny. It's good because some of the others, they are too serious.'

'Why? What do you talk about, when you are together?'

'Just the past,' Dad says. 'Always the past: about Poland, the camp, Russia. We never talk about here.' Then he's silent for a moment, as if digesting his own observation for the first time. 'You know, it's as if what has happened all this time in New Zealand, all those years of work and family, this isn't important to them. Only the past is important. If you think about it, it's very strange.'

~

In the damp, bone-aching cold of Lublin, the past was everywhere. On cobbled streets, overlooked by stone buildings, I'd felt the cheer drip away, like the freezing water trickling from my raincoat hood. Even the arrival of our noisy family convoy had failed to lift that Polish city's stubborn greyness. The children were shuffling and grizzling on the edges of our family huddle, hands shoved in pockets and heads bowed. The guide's voice had finally lost its smile. It was as if, for the first time, she also understood just how bleak the city's stories of loss really were. Lublin, she told us, with its strategic location on an important trade route, had a long history of invasion and destruction; many aggressive neighbours had laid claim to it over the centuries. But not all the brutality was ancient. In my father's lifetime, the Nazi invaders had permanently destroyed the Jewish pulse of the city. And while I'd been growing up elsewhere, oblivious, the social revolt against the post-war communist regime had its beginnings in rallies on Lublin's narrow streets and in mass strikes on its factory floors. The city's misery was unrelenting, like the rain. I wondered if this was what my father had been talking about a week earlier, the night before we left for Poland. In the bar of our Dubai hotel, he'd said he didn't want to go any more.

'It's not the same,' he announced to Alicja and me. 'It's not the Poland I remember.'

We had flown to Dubai from Tehran only that morning and our Iranian experience already seemed hazy, a little like the dusty orange sunset we were watching over the desert city's outskirts. I had a drink in my hand, and my head was scarf-free. On a low mirrored table between us sat a bowl of olives and a bundle of paper cocktail napkins. 'I'd be just as happy to go home now,' Dad said. 'I loved Iran.'

I caught Alicja's look and rolled my eyes. We would be going to Poland tomorrow and Dad would be coming with us. Everything was arranged and had been for months: James, Anna, Jeremy and Lucy would meet us there, along with Alicja's brother Stefan and his 20-year-old daughter Marianna. We would spend Easter with Wojtek and his family and then travel together to Kraków and eastern Poland. I was looking forward to it. But my father's reluctance was new; I'd never thought he'd lose interest in his homeland.

Now, a week later in Lublin, my daughter Lucy was slipping her cold hand into mine in my jacket pocket. 'Can we get pancakes? I'm hungry.'

'That would be good,' Dad said, from behind me. 'I've had enough.'

He was wearing the oilskin cap with earflaps that I'd bought him for Christmas years ago, but he looked miserable. Damp shadows were spreading across his jacket shoulders and he kicked at a loose cobble under his foot. 'And I can't hear what that woman is saying.' I tried to suppress a surge of impatience. Lublin was only 120 kilometres away from where my father was born; its historic centre was original, almost unscathed by its terrible wartime history. I thought he'd like to visit a Polish city—perhaps the only one—that still looked much as it would have when he lived nearby. But my father never came here as a child, I realised. He didn't know this city at all then, and he wasn't interested in it now.

When we found a brick-lined restaurant off Lublin's central square, everyone's mood improved. The waiter led us to a large square table near an open fire; Monika and I arranged our damp raincoats like flags around its glow. Monika was the Kraków-based guide I'd met on a previous trip who had agreed to shepherd us through eastern Poland in this two-vehicle convoy. She'd organised our itinerary in return for a small fee and expenses, and I was increasingly pleased to have her unflappable company and trouble-shooting assistance. We were a noisy and happy group of 10 again.

'Look Dziadzio,' Lucy said to her grandfather, who was smiling again, 'the menu comes in English too!'

But later, back at our hotel near the old castle, an old nunnery, my father's good mood evaporated. He'd had enough of the ghosts of dead kings, protestors, and Jews. He wanted to go to Dobrynka tomorrow. 'It's on the way north,' he said, perched on the edge of his single bed. 'Why can't we go there?'

'Because we talked about this already, months ago, and we'd decided not to visit Dobrynka again,' I said.

'Okay. It's up to you. You're in charge.'

'It's not about who's in charge, Dad. It's about what everybody wants to do, about what's already been organised. Stuff that you agreed to.'

'Okay,' he said, 'it's up to you.'

At six o'clock, on Lublin's freezing streets, my father went missing.

Outside the nunnery, nine people waited for him on stone steps in the drizzle, the hoods of our jackets up. I'm hungry, one of the children said. Where's Dziadzio? At the nunnery's poky reception desk, a puzzled woman with greying curls was reluctant to part with a key to his room. No, he wasn't answering his phone. Yes, we had tried knocking. What if he was ill? But my father's room was indeed empty, his comb and lotions arranged neatly beneath the dressing table mirror and its hovering crucifix. 'He's just sulking,' I said to my cousin. 'It's because we're not going to Dobrynka tomorrow. He's taken off somewhere.'

Outside, in the drizzle, it was getting colder. The restaurant booking was for 6 p.m. and Monika was getting anxious.

'Did your father know what time we were meeting?' she asked me. 'Why would he go away if he knew this was when we were meeting?'

I didn't know how to explain it to her: that my father had always worked to his own timetable. That it was normal for him to disappear on his own like that without explanation, for a walk, an errand or, sometimes, for no reason at all. That when I was a child, so many family outings—at the races in Tauranga, the Easter Show in Auckland, family picnics to the beach—had been defined by this mysterious vanishing and then the oddly tense boredom of waiting for his return. He would return, eventually, hands in pockets, to be greeted with my mother's sulky silence. But she wasn't there to disapprove today. This disappearance, I realised, was for my benefit.

Ten minutes later, the shuffling figure of my father appeared in the streetlights, head bowed under his damp cap, a plastic bag dangling from his hand. He was surprised by the fuss. He'd gone to a shop to buy vodka for tomorrow. What was the matter with us? He was hungry. What were we doing for dinner?

~

I'd visited Dobrynka only once before, on my first visit to Poland in 1988. Even then, it hadn't been much more than a smudged mark on our foldout map of Eastern Poland, a pencilled X my uncle had made to help me navigate the featureless landscape. I remembered no landmarks in the area at all: no folksy collection of houses or shops, no church, no welcome sign to indicate we had arrived. I remembered only an unremarkable house on a road that seemed to run in an endless straight line to the flat horizon.

We'd arrived late in the afternoon, speeding through narrow country lanes lined on each side with soldier-like birch trees, our Renault hatchback slowing only to negotiate the rough cobbles of village streets or the occasional horse-drawn cart. It was late afternoon, still warm and sunny. Wacek, squeezed in the centre of the back seat between Jasia and Kazik, his face shiny in the heat, had shouted enthusiastic directions to me in Polish. '*Prawo*, Helena. *Prawo!*' Our exact destination seemed to be a mystery to everyone in the car except for Wacek. My father was also unable to explain.

'Some relatives of mine,' he had said, when I asked. 'I think maybe my cousin.'

The house we arrived at was painted a fading olive green, its window frames peeling brown. It wasn't unlike the sad roadside dwellings we had passed the previous few days. Rural Poland, after more than 40 years under communist Soviet rule, was scenic, but its infrastructure was clearly neglected and decaying. As I pulled up on the grass behind a rusting Polski Fiat I looked at my passengers for further instructions. Why this house? Wacek had already climbed from his seat to greet a group of people who had appeared along the bald footpaths that curled through the long grass. My uncle was greeted warmly—yes, we had come to the right place—and then, from all directions, children arrived. They ran around the car, barefoot, squealing and stroking its shiny headlights and panels. One by one, oldest to youngest, we were introduced to each member of the household. Amid the colourful parade of Polish babble, I began losing track of the hands I shook and cheeks kissed: who were all these people?

'*Dzień dobry*,' I said to a stooped old lady wearing a headscarf who held me by my shoulders and leaned close to say something I couldn't understand.

'What did she say? Who is she?' I asked my father.

'I don't know. Maybe my aunt?'

When prodded to take part in the introductions, the children became wary. The boys, wearing too-small T-shirts tucked into shorts, and the girls, in gathered floral skirts, held out their hands shyly. Some were close to my age; one carried a round-faced and dribbling baby, also wearing a tiny headscarf, on her hip.

'Is this her baby?' I asked my father, 'or her little sister?' He shrugged again, clearly irritated now by my constant need for translation and explanation.

'No idea, I've got no idea.'

We were ushered inside and through a dim passageway to the main room of the house. A wooden table that had been set against one wall was pulled into the centre. Chickens scattered from beneath it, their claws scratching on the torn linoleum as they fled. Chairs were fetched and one of the girls spread a worn floral cloth over the table's surface. Another gathered mismatched crockery from a glass-fronted and wobbly sideboard. I tried not to stare at the pages from German magazines glued to one of the room's walls, a collage that I guessed was an attempt to provide some colour to the room. These bikini-clad models and Michael Jackson's face were to become the backdrop to our impromptu party.

I took it all in from my corner seat at that busy table: the steady flow of loud Polish conversation and laughter, the shots of vodka poured into odd-sized glasses and tumblers, the endless plates of halved boiled eggs, sliced homemade salami and gherkins that appeared in the hands of one female relative after another. The central figure in the household—the person who was Wacek's connection—was a woman called Maria, possibly

The house in Dobrynka, Poland, in which Stefan's father, Józef, was born in 1880. Above, in 1988, with Jasia, Genowefa, Wacek, Kazik, Stefan and Zbigniew; below, in 2012, with Maria, Zbigniew and Stefan.

the same age as my mother, her wiry brown curls beginning to grey and her body round and matronly. Her husband, Zbigniew, wore a singlet stretched tight over his belly, and his dark moustache drooped to points on either side of his chin. The cigarette he held between the yellowed fingers of his right hand was tapped continuously into an ashtray on the tablecloth. The family farmed here, my father eventually told me, on the land that had been Wiśniewski property before the war, land that had once been worked by Maria's father, Franek, my great-uncle. But as the sky darkened outside and the volume in the room increased, my father seemed to forget I was there. I knew I was sometimes the subject of discussion, but I couldn't decipher its ebb and flow. Dad had stopped translating, only occasionally dragging me into the conversation by speaking directly to me in Polish and dissolving into giggles at his error. I didn't need to understand the dialogue to recognise the droop in his eyes, the shine and flush on his cheeks—he was drunk. It was his fault, I decided, that I couldn't speak Polish. He owed me some effort.

'I can't keep up with two conversations, there's too much going on,' he said, brushing me off when I interrupted at one point to complain. 'I'll tell you tomorrow.'

Worse still, it seemed we would be staying at this house. I'd already learned there was no bathroom, only an outhouse, and there was no sign of beds or bedrooms. Where would we sleep? In the end, we slept on the floor of the room. The table was pushed to one side again and mattresses appeared with blankets and pillows lined up for the five visitors. I lay awake, angry and uncomfortable, listening to my father's and my uncles' noisy, wet snoring. What was it about vodka that seemed to incite that mawkish homesickness in my father's family? Viewed in the gloom of the night, from my lumpy pillow on the floor, this room was as foreign as any I'd ever been in. I couldn't believe that this place and the people who lived here were connected to me. More confusing was the complete ease I'd seen in my father that day. Was it only the vodka and his comfort with the language that had made him so relaxed among these strangers? Or was there something else that I had missed, something that had fallen through the father-daughter gap between us?

Before we left the following morning, we posed with our hosts for photographs in dazzling morning sunshine. I'd wanted to take the photos in front of the green house. Maria insisted we also take some in front of the dark wooden shack by the gate. I hadn't noticed it the night before, this little building with its sawn log walls, steep thatched roof and single window. Now I learned that this shed, filled with hay and empty barrels, was where my grandfather Józef had been born in 1880.

'So you can tell me now, all about it,' I said to Dad later, as we drove away.

'About what?' He was quiet, sitting in the passenger seat beside me, staring at the fields that were quickly disappearing behind us. My uncles and aunt, in the back seat, were chatting in Polish. 'What are you talking about?'

'About where we've just been. About who all those people were.'

'Well, I don't know. I can't remember. I think they were my relatives, my cousins or something.' He looked out the window again for a moment and then turned back to me.

'But wasn't it amazing?' he said. 'Wasn't it such a wonderful thing?'

～

Twenty-five years later, in a nunnery in Lublin, my cousin Stefan offered to take my father back to Dobrynka.

'It's nice of you,' I said to him, 'but don't let Dad push you into things.'

'No, it's fine,' he said. 'It might be interesting. I might learn something.'

Stefan, like his sister Alicja, was the best kind of travelling companion: even-tempered and happy to compromise. The second of Alicja's three younger brothers, Stefan had been the practical child in a household of sporty and academic high-achievers. His basement bedroom in their Pakuranga home had been littered with the old toasters and cassette players that he repeatedly took apart and reassembled; I'd thought him impressive as a teenager. Now a middle-aged father in an era of high-tech electronics, my cousin was still a traditional fix-it man. My father, the uncle he was named after, seemed unaware that the detour to Dobrynka would add another two hours' driving to an already long travel day. Alicja and I would drive with Dad and Stefan; James, Monika and the children, meanwhile, would stick to the original route and meet us further north later that night. In the freezing morning drizzle, suitcases and coats were moved between vehicles in the hotel car park, while Dad and the children watched us silently from under the hotel's eaves. When we reached a busy intersection just outside Lublin's centre we took different routes. Their van went north, our car northeast, and I saw Lucy's hands waving to me through rain-fogged windows. As the vehicle faded from view, lost in a wet smear of red tail lights, I wondered why I wasn't with them.

Within an hour, Lublin's weekday streets gave way to single-lane roads between damp villages. Storks were nesting on lamp posts, poking murky outlines into the sky. Wooden shrines dotted in flat fields offered travellers religious sanctuary and colourful shelter: candles, plastic flowers, a wooden chair or two, Madonna and Child paintings. But my father didn't seem interested in these quaint symbols of rural Poland. He sighed when we stopped to look, impatiently rubbing his hands up and down on his thighs.

217

'It's no good for photos today, the light's no good. And the people in the houses are watching us.'

He was right: the storks seen through our camera lenses were just spiky shadows, and curtains in village windows were twitching. But his impatience annoyed me. He had talked my cousin into this detour and it was clear that the closer we got to our destination, the less confident he was of a successful outcome. For a start, we had no address in Dobrynka. Like me, Dad remembered only the little green house from 25 years ago, its outhouse and chickens, not its location. He couldn't remember the family's surname; we knew only that it wasn't Wiśniewski. Even if we found the house, there was no guarantee anyone would be home; there was no guarantee the family still lived there at all. So we went instead to the nearest town, Piszczac, where crows called from misty trees outside the village church, and where Dad decided to ask the local priest for help. I watched him from the car as he crossed the road from the church to the presbytery. A thin path led from the gate to the house, its windows unlit. He knocked and then put his hands back in his pockets, waiting. I was impressed by this uncharacteristic determination. The father I knew was wary about approaching strangers for help and would be the first to encourage others not to bother. But he reappeared from the presbytery with a spring in his step. The priest had invited us in. His grumpy housekeeper made us tea in the steamy kitchen while our relatives were called.

We were still sipping tea and lemon when they arrived, a jumble of Polish noise and kisses, in gaudy cardigans and leather jackets. It was only Maria whose name I remembered; the others smiled at me with familiar but hazy faces. Let's go to the cemetery, they said.

~

It was Maria who led us to the graves. As we picked our way through the maze of tightly packed headstones I established that the other women in the group were Maria's daughters; was I imagining things, or did I remember two smiling, dark-haired girls from my first visit? The man with them was Maria's son-in-law, the local photographer, who wore a large camera slung around his neck like a mayoral chain. But none of our guides spoke English and my father was once again unwilling to be translator.

'Which sister is married to the photographer?' I asked him as we walked.

'I can't work it out,' he said. 'I'll have to tell you later.'

At the family plot, we arranged ourselves around the two headstones decorated with colourful glass hurricane lamps and faded plastic flowers. One grave belonged to Franek, my great uncle, Maria's father. On the same headstone was a more recent inscription for his wife, Genowefa, who, I now learned, was the old lady I remembered from my previous visit, Maria's mother. Genowefa had died in 2008 aged 100. Next to Maria's parents' shared headstone was her grandparents' grave, the same grandparents my father never met, and whose names I had never heard before: Wilhelm and Joanna Wiśniewski.

The name Wilhelm was a shock. It wasn't Polish. Why would my great grandfather have a German Christian name?

'What do you think?' I asked Alicja quietly on the way to Maria's home. 'Could they have been German?' I knew that Poland's fluid and disputed boundaries were centuries old, and that less than 100 years earlier the country hadn't existed on any map, partitioned and absorbed into its neighbours' boundaries. Dobrynka had been part of the Russian Empire in those years, the border of East Prussia not far to the north. With the abolition of serfdom in Russia in 1862, several hundred thousand Germans had migrated to the eastern borderlands to work for

Polish landlords. It was quite possible that some of my ancestors were once German migrants; it had just never occurred to me that they would be. On our way, Dad chatted happily to one of Maria's daughters. He clearly wasn't bothered by the discovery. I would ask him later, I decided.

Despite the 25-year interval between this visit and our last, Maria and her husband were generous and accommodating again. We received the same noisy welcome, the same hugs and handshakes. The family now had a new concrete block home next to the old house, this one with an indoor toilet and double-glazed windows. The chickens were gone, as was the wallpaper made from the pages of magazines, but I was sure we sat around the same wooden table in their crowded living room and drank from the same mismatched glasses. In the babble of Polish conversation, I could see Maria's robustness and her farmer husband's toughness had given way to old age; they were more subdued and watchful than I remembered. It was their daughters, now middle-aged like me, who carried plates of food and bottles of vodka to the table.

Maria rolled her shot glass thoughtfully between her fingers, smiling while my father told a long, animated story in Polish. Maybe she, too, was thinking about the yawning gap of history between our visits, the losses and the gains of those years. The fall of communist Poland didn't appear to have transformed her family's fortunes so much as shifted them slightly sideways. Perhaps the country's capitalist transformation—the rise of Solidarity, the first free elections, Poland's new democratic constitution and its rebirth as the 'Third Polish Republic'—had simply left villages like Dobrynka behind. This was the same isolated rural community I remembered from my first visit, a relic of a sad history, but maybe one that was more aware of its shortcomings than it used to be. My relatives' lives still seemed to be playing out on the fringes of poverty. The world at the end of the long road heading west—the exotic place we had come from—was just as out of reach for them as it had always been.

The grey was fading to black when we left. My father, in the back seat next to me, made an announcement. He wanted to thank his nephew, Stefan, who'd driven him to Dobrynka, even though nobody else wanted to go. It had been wonderful, he said, just fantastic. From the driver's seat, my cousin smiled and glanced sympathetically at me in the rear vision mirror.

'That's okay, Uncle Stefan,' he said, 'it was interesting.'

My father hadn't said anything to me since we left. His head had been firmly turned away to the darkening fields outside. This was the Poland he missed, I realised. Dobrynka, with its patchwork fields and colourful cemeteries, was like the childhood Brześć he remembered. It had been frozen in time just for him; it still wore the fingerprints of his history. Had my father's house in 1939 been a few kilometres west on the 'right' side of the Bug River, and not in Soviet-occupied Brześć, he would never have been deported. If he hadn't been deported and deposited by chance on islands on the other side of the world, Maria's life here might have been his. The other Poland—modern, urban Poland with its graffiti, pancake parlours and international airports—was as alien to him as Siberia had once been.

'So Dad,' I said, 'what do you think about having German grandparents?'

'What?' my father said, surprised I had spoken to him. 'What are you talking about?'

'The graves we visited today, your grandparents' graves. Wilhelm doesn't sound like a Polish name.'

'No, no,' my father said. 'They're not my grandparents, not in those graves.'

'Who are they then?'

'I don't know.' He looked at the blackness outside again. 'I don't know about everything.'

I didn't have the energy to argue with him. I'd show him the evidence, the photos of the headstones we visited, tomorrow. But he was clearly, and unusually for him, still annoyed with me. I'd let him down somehow and despite the day's happy outcome I was not going to be forgiven that night. My reference to the potential German ancestry in the family probably hadn't helped, but it had also confirmed he hadn't absorbed a lot of what we'd seen that day. Maybe it was all too much, too overwhelming, this rerun of our previous visit.

Outside, I saw another cemetery wheeling past through the darkness. Hundreds of orange hurricane lamps glowed like pretty headlights in the night and then were gone. These Polish sites of mourning reminded me of the colourful Pacific Island cemeteries of home, where anniversaries of deceased loved ones were celebrated in cheerful symmetry with those of the living. I was hundreds of kilometres from any ocean, thousands of kilometres from an ocean that was familiar to me, and I was suddenly homesick. Maria and her family were living the simple lives of my ancestors, but this place wasn't mine.

I understood my father's wartime exile was a tragedy for him; I knew now it was a blessing for me. I was standing on the banks of a summery Bug River again, my flatmate's words from 25 years ago ringing in my ears. 'Things always fall into place for you. You're just a lucky person.'

11

I walked delicately as a butterfly
And heavily as an elephant,
I walked surely as a dancer
And wavered like a blind man.
I didn't believe that I would cross that bridge,
And now that I am standing on the other side,
I don't believe I crossed it.

Leopold Staff, 'The Bridge'

The day Zofia turns 50, we decide to walk. She's waiting for me at the rise at the end of our street, and I recognise her silhouette long before I get there. A dark-haired outline in a navy sleeveless vest, she lifts one hand to me in greeting, swinging a plastic water bottle between her fingers.

'Happy birthday Zof,' I say. 'How does it feel?'

'Thanks,' she says, smiling, 'it feels fine.'

Only the occasion of my sister's birthday makes this rendezvous anything other than ordinary. Our lives still track with a symmetry that has never seemed deliberate, but is too neat to be accidental. We live in the same suburb, have children who are friends, and have the same ageing parents in whom we see more of ourselves every day. It's not just the way we look, the droop around the eyes and chin, but the way we move. My sister, I notice now, shares Mum's rolling gait, its tip and sway. And maybe my father's legacy is there too. The act of walking, this urge Zofia and I both seem to have to put one foot slowly in front of another, to make circles around the boundaries of home, is something we have inherited from him.

I walk most days, sometimes with a friend, sometimes with my sister. My father still walks alone. He's too fast for my mother—Mum walks unsteadily now, almost fearfully— and too slow for me. His solo encounters with the world are more leisurely than they once were, but they are regular and purposeful. If Mum hasn't got plans, an appointment or coffee date, she waits at home for him in the mornings, pacing around their townhouse, busy with nothing in particular, until he arrives home with stories to share over lunch. In the Botanic Garden, Dad likes to hover near the tourists who gather at the city's viewpoints near the top of the cable car. They are always happy to chat, he says, and unlike the locals, 'are not so much in a hurry.' On the city's waterfront, another favourite route, he regularly passes the plaque commemorating the arrival of the Polish children in 1944. Beneath the ubiquitous Polish Eagle, the Poles' gratitude is immortalised in raised brass lettering: 'They became self-sufficient, hard-working, loyal citizens and ... they say thank you to the New Zealand Government, the New Zealand Army, Catholic Church, caregivers, teachers and all who extended a helping hand.' Then, in a flourish of capitals, the text finishes: 'Thanks to you all, and God Bless. *Bóg Zapłać.*'

'I saw some people there, at the plaque, today,' he reported over lunch recently. A guide had been explaining the story of the Polish children to a group of tourists, probably from a visiting cruise ship, while he'd hovered at the back of the group, listening.

'He was telling them that the Polish children were World War II immigrants. So I called out from the back and said, "Excuse me, but you're wrong, the Polish children were not immigrants. We didn't choose to leave Poland. The New Zealand government *invited* the Polish children here, for the duration of the war. This is a big difference." And then the man, he said to me: "How do you know this?" and I said, "Because I'm one of them."'

I imagined my father, his hands pushed deep in his jacket pockets, rocking back on his heels, as the tourists in white shoes and with tags around their necks turned slowly to look at him.

'It was quite funny,' he said, his mouth full of sandwich, 'the way they reacted. They all wanted to shake my hand then and have a photo. Actually, I quite enjoyed it.'

Today, to start her birthday celebrations, my sister and I climb bush-lined tracks rutted by the weekend's mountain bikers to another World War II reminder. This one, at the summit of Karori's Wright's Hill, is not a post-dated plaque, but the real thing: a fortress built in 1942 to protect Wellington from feared Japanese invasion.

While we climb, we talk about the tension between Mum and Dad over recent months, about her threats to send him back to Siberia, about how there seem to be signs of a thaw, even some kindnesses between them. Last night, in a room full of family at Zofia's early birthday dinner, I'd watched our parents talking, heads bent together, deep in shared understanding of an issue of little interest to anyone else.

'Maybe it's the change in weather,' Zofia suggests. 'Or maybe it was the vodka.'

I laugh, but I know there's more to it than that. Our parents' relationship is still as perplexing to us as it was when we were children caught in its random crossfire. As far as I know, Mum hasn't discussed her latest family discoveries with my father. Maxim Gorky and Joseph's socialist tattoo are pieces of a past that she's not yet willing—or brave enough—to share with him. My father, for his part, still disappears every Sunday to Polish Mass without her. I wonder, though, if any of that matters. My research, the travel, this story about him: all of it is inconceivable without her. They have been married for more than half a century; she is there through all of it. The little Jewish girl in my father's playground has Olga's eyes. The empty seat between us on the plane is hers. Perhaps my parents have simply done their job so well that Zofia and I forget we are the daughters of not one but two damaged people: one a child exiled and the other a child abandoned. And we have our own marriages to think about now, with children who are probably just as puzzled by their parents' inexplicable domestic behaviour. Maybe we should offer our parents more sympathy, even gratitude, than we have in the past.

At the summit, a stiff southerly wind lifts the hair from our necks and we don't linger over the familiar view of steely harbour and sky. Instead, we make our way towards the road, past the now empty gun emplacement, a deep crater dug into the hilltop plateau. The gun that was once there was never needed in action; the Japanese didn't invade as feared. It was fired only once, a year after the war ended, and as an exercise of curiosity rather than necessity. As the test shot arced over Wellington's gorse-covered southern hills and out into the wilderness of Cook Strait, eager defence force officials measured its fall. According to army reports, the experiment was 'most satisfactory'. Then the gun, its untapped value established, was sold as scrap metal to the former enemy Japanese. All that's left of the fortress is the hole on this hill and a maze of underground tunnels that network pointlessly under our feet. I remember being in them once with Jeremy, when he was little, when they were unlocked and open to the public. My blond son joined the dozens of children who ricocheted through the tunnels, shrieking in mock terror, as if pursued by the ghosts of the men who had once worked so hard to build them.

It's a relief to be able to smile when I walk past this quaint memorial of war. How much easier it is to step over these innocent tunnels than on the dead grass and bloodstained rubble of that other fortress in Brest, my father's hometown. Here in Wellington, there's nothing to mourn, no skulls to kick.

Here, my children are free to forget. Brass plaques of thanks are not required. And my sister and I can keep marching, without guilt or a backward glance, on our way to coffee, on our way home.

~

'Why did you call me Helena?' I ask my parents.

'I've told you,' Dad says, 'we named you after my sister. She was my favourite sister, she understood me, she was my biggest supporter.'

'I wanted Stefania,' Mum says, before my father can say anything more. 'But I didn't want Izabela; Isabella was my stepmother's name.'

My father is silenced by this outburst. He looks at my mother, then at me.

'What's wrong with Helena? It's a good name. It sounds like English, so it's good for New Zealand.'

'But it's always so mispronounced,' I complain. 'Hel-*ay*-na, Hel-*ee*-na, Hel-en-*a* . . . it's a nightmare name.'

'You know there are lots of other ways of saying it, don't you? Helenka, Helushka, Hela,' he says. 'I know, how about from now on I call you Hela? Hela's easy, not confusing.'

I'm surprised by the lurch I feel, a sudden wave of thumping panic.

'No, not Hela,' I say. 'Not Hela. Don't call me Hela.'

~

To begin with, Hela and Henek's house in Coronation Road, Papatoetoe, was the centre of Wiśniewski family life in New Zealand. Hela would host Christmas Eve celebrations for her siblings in its dining room, and a bed in the back sunroom

Zofia's baptism, Coronation Road, Papatoetoe, 1964. Adults, from left to right: Kazik, Hela, Barbara, Olga, Alina, Bolek, Iza, Henek.
To begin with, Hela and Henek's house was the centre of Wiśniewski family life in New Zealand.

Hela in the sunroom at Coronation Road, 1960s.
And it smells, I swear, of Hela's Palmolive house and the little sunroom by the kitchen where she kept her unfinished stitching under the hinged lid of the window seat.

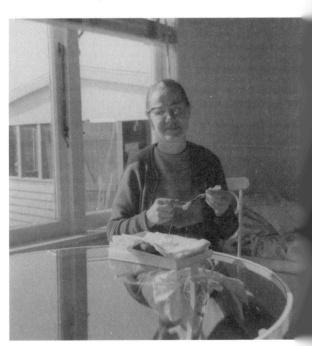

was available for those, like my father, who were occasionally between homes and jobs. The house became a showcase for the decorated Polish war veteran and his new bride, its small living room deliberately decorated for formal entertaining, not relaxed family living. Iza laughs as she remembers Hela choosing every piece of her living room furniture—'the chairs, the lamps and curtains, that terrible clock'—from a window display she'd admired in Queen Street's upmarket department store, Milne and Choyce.

The girls, both at business college, had moved in with their older sister and her husband when they'd finished school. 'We didn't have a choice,' Iza says. 'We didn't have anywhere else to go.' They became home help for Hela and kitchen hands for when she and her husband entertained Polish visitors. The couple entertained a lot in the early days of their marriage, mostly older dignitaries from the Polish community and visitors from overseas. 'It was just expected that we worked when we were there. Henek always reminded us that we had to be grateful for everything, for what they had given up for us.'

Despite appearances, Hela and her husband weren't wealthy. Both worked long hours in tedious physical jobs. Henek, who'd arrived in Tasmania describing himself as a labourer— and whose hands and fingernails were impeccably clean and manicured throughout his life, despite the grimy nature of his work—became a metal grinder. 'I've never know anyone who worked as hard as him,' Dad says. 'He would work every scrap of overtime he could get. He would never turn work down. And it was terrible work, noisy and dirty, filing away at the rough edges of machinery all day. It would have driven me mad.' Hela, meanwhile, was a machinist at the nearby Bendon factory in Papatoetoe and was as determined as her husband to maintain appearances at all cost. Iza remembers cleaning the house at the weekends so that her older sister could work while Henek worked overtime himself. 'If we cleaned the house it would look as if Hela had been home,' she says. 'She didn't want Henek to know that she was working extra hours.'

Life changed for everyone when my younger aunts married their respective husbands—Polish boys they met through my father. 'When I got engaged to Mietek, all I could think was, my God, now I can live my own life,' Iza says. 'It was a wonderful feeling.' It had been my father, rather than Hela, who'd been the real guardian in those years, she says. Stefan was working in Auckland at the time, and he'd kept a close eye on his younger sisters. He'd vetted all the Polish boys who'd asked his younger sisters out, advising them on boys to keep away from and those to encourage. 'We were very innocent, Alina and I,' Iza says, 'and Stefan always looked after us as far as men were concerned.' This is a side of my father I have never seen; his opinion of my teenage boyfriends was never shared with me. I'd always assumed his silence implied his approval, but perhaps he simply didn't know what to think. Perhaps the world in which his daughters were growing up, its freedoms and its dangers, was too inexplicable to evaluate.

Iza and Alina's double wedding—'we had it together because it was cheaper that way'—was held several months after my parents' marriage in 1959. It marked the end of a chapter for Hela. All her siblings were married and she was no longer responsible for their welfare.

~

No one can now say when Hela first showed signs of being unwell.

My mother had always felt welcomed by her older sister-in-law—'she was very fond of your father, so she was always good to me'—but she remembers one Christmas Eve at Coronation

Road, in the early years of their marriage, where the evening turned to chaos. 'Everything was overcooked, there was stuff all over the place,' Mum says. 'The rest of the family was horrified, they were all talking about it.' Another year, soon after, Hela served everybody ice blocks.

'That was it, just flavoured ice blocks,' Iza says. 'We sat there eating them at the dining table and then went back to my place. I think we didn't have Christmas at Coronation Road again.'

Hela's behaviour became increasingly erratic, her religious fervour intense. At family social events, she would stand with her back to a wall, silent and staring. At Mass she would ignore the congregation's combined movements and sit, kneel and stand at whim. Henek was out of his depth, paralysed by his wife's transformation, unable to communicate with doctors. Iza and Alina took over arranging doctor's appointments and medication, most of which their sister refused or neglected to take. She seemed to be hearing voices, and would disappear from home for extended periods, walking, as my parents were to find out, further than anyone could believe. Sometimes these disappearances bore echoes of the traumatic past Hela had clearly been unable to put behind her. One day she appeared at the door of Alina's Manurewa home, more than seven kilometres from Coronation Road, with a sack of potatoes on her back. Alicja, too, recalls Hela arriving at their Pakuranga home one summer afternoon. Her aunt had clearly walked the 12-kilometre distance from Papatoetoe in the afternoon heat. She was red-faced and sweating, wearing her coat, gloves and hat.

'I think Mum and Dad were both at work,' Alicja says. 'It was quite scary encountering her like this.'

Hela was eventually disgnosed with schizophrenia, and she received electro-convulsive therapy throughout the 1970s at Kingseat Hospital in Karaka, south of Auckland. Each time she reached a low point and Henek was no longer able to cope with her at home, an ambulance was called. Iza remembers the screaming, my aunt clawing at doorframes, begging not to be taken away. And after each treatment and extended hospital stay Hela would be transformed, at least for a while, to something near her old self. 'She would thank me, afterwards, for making her go,' Iza says now. 'She was grateful.'

I have one other fuzzy memory from Hela's bad years: a visit with my family to see her, not in her quiet house in Papatoetoe, but in Kingseat's beautiful gardens. Through the Hillman's rear window as we'd arrived, I'd been entranced by the romantic tree-lined driveway, the building revealing itself slowly, like a stately home from the opening shots of a TV documentary. I couldn't believe this magical place was a hospital. Twenty years later, Kingseat closed, a casualty of government policy and changing attitudes to psychiatric care. Within five years of its closure in 1999, more than 200 former patients of this and other New Zealand psychiatric institutions had filed complaints of mistreatment and abuse during the 1960s and 70s. Hela, who'd been a patient in those years, had died in 1992, and her opinion of her treatment there remains a mystery. But I wonder what she would think of the slow decay of the grand and secluded buildings I remember.

Today, tourists and day-trippers, not patients, wander through the hospital's once-carefully tended shrubberies, flowerbeds and trees grown from the seeds of George Grey's garden on Kawau Island. The former nurses' home on the site has a dubious new reputation: it's the location of more than 100 reported sightings of ghosts and apparitions, and the country's 'most haunted' building. Visitors can play 'Asylum Paintball' in its grounds, or, if they wish, go to the country's only 'Haunted Attraction Scream Park' indoors. Here, the publicity tells me, 'mutated living half men, souls of the damned, and bloody corpses of the undead lie in waiting. Restless and hungry, these creatures of the night will have no mercy upon you.'

Even in death, I decide, the former inhabitants of that sad institution will not be allowed peace. For them, too, there will be no mercy.

~

The Polish children, New Zealand's first formal refugee group, have been scrutinised for 70 years. Sociologists and psychologists have tried to define the challenges they faced making lives for themselves in this country, some describing it as 'the shock of displacement', others as a 'severe psychological experience in adjustment'. The children, it seems, were tough; they were already hardened survivors when they arrived, and the struggles of adjustment didn't stop many of them from leading successful adult lives in New Zealand. This, perhaps, would have been the more valuable study: why did so few fail when the odds had been so stacked against them?

By 1955, ten years after the war ended, 82 of the 732 Polish children had left New Zealand, returning to uncertain futures and broken families in a communist Poland. 'The children I knew who went back,' Iza says, 'lots of them didn't do so well. We were lucky we stayed.' Of those still in New Zealand in 1955, about 10 percent had achieved School Certificate, and a smaller number University Entrance. Three had university degrees. In 1965, ten years later, the Polish women seemed to be doing better overall, at least in terms of work. Only 18 percent were unskilled. The majority, among them my three aunts, were clerical or skilled workers. The youngest, Alina—perhaps jolted into action by her older sister's earlier disappointments in education—was the only Wiśniewski sibling who had passed School Certificate. Of the Polish men, more than 40 percent were unskilled labourers and only 29 percent were, like my father and his brother, skilled workers or tradesmen.

Most of the Polish children were nonetheless leading independent lives. The Wiśniewski siblings were married, several with children of their own. The statistics gathered in later decades showed that almost 700 Polish-born men and women married in New Zealand between the war and the mid-60s. Many men married Polish women but a greater percentage married New Zealanders. The trend was reversed for women: the far greater percentage of Polish-born women married Poles. The community encouraged marriage between Poles, seeing it as a way to keep the culture strong in New Zealand. In Wellington, where more than half of them lived, Polish enclaves emerged, concentrated in the southern suburbs and the Hutt Valley. My friend Marysia grew up in one of those communities in Island Bay, her family's life circling around a tight and perhaps reassuring ritual of Polish Mass, Polish school, Polish friends.

It was also clear, even as early as the mid-1960s, that some of the now-adult orphans were not coping at all. A study published in the early 70s, and one that upset many members of the Polish community at the time, showed some evidence—arguably unsurprising—of mental illness among the survivors. Only 282 orphans remained on the Aliens Register in 1966 (those naturalised before that date were excluded). Of those, 6.4 percent had entered psychiatric institutions as voluntary or involuntary patients since 1950. This statistic would have included my aunt. And two thirds of these patients were among the older group— the children who, like my father and Hela, had been teenagers on arrival in 1944. It seemed it was the older children who had found it more difficult to let go of the horrors and losses of their wartime past and adjust to the prospect of life in a country a long way from home.

Maybe, my father says, it was his marriage to my mother,

a non-Pole, that helped him settle. Olga was happy in New Zealand; she would help him learn how to be comfortable here too.

'And maybe it was a good thing that we lived in Whakatane, in a place with none of my old Polish friends,' he says. 'Maybe I couldn't think so much about the past like the other Poles, the ones who stayed together. I had to get on with it and make a life. So that's what I did. I made a life.'

~

Henek died in 1999, seven years after his wife. Iza and Mietek made it their job to look after him in those years, and were regular visitors to the rest home he moved to once Coronation Road became unmanageable. He spent many hours, they say, sitting alone on the bench at a nearby bus stop, watching passing traffic. As they tell me about my uncle's final years, it dawns on me how little thought I gave to Hela's husband, the war hero who was the source of so much amusement to me throughout my childhood and whose face had faded from view as I became an adult. Henek, after almost 40 years in New Zealand, could speak only a little English when he died. He was still a foreigner in this country; he would have been as lonely and unhappy here as his wife.

But it is Hela who still haunts my father's memories.

'Hela was my best friend,' Dad says, this unexpected declaration silencing our recollections of her husband. 'Well she stood up for me, all the time. She understood what I was going through when I was young. Nobody else did. And I was with her, just me, when she died.'

A few months after my wedding in 1991, my parents visited Hela and Henek at Coronation Road. Hela had seemed quite well, her schizophrenia finally under control with a new drug regime. She was lucid, if a little quiet. But when the visitors stood to leave, Hela took Dad by the arm and pulled him towards her as they passed through the little galley kitchen to the back door.

'She put her face, just here,' Dad says, stroking the swoop of the curve between his neck and left shoulder, 'and she leaned right into me. And then she said, "There's something wrong Stefan. I'm not right. There's something wrong."'

Something had been 'wrong' with Hela almost all her adult life, but my father knew she wasn't referring to her mental illness. The diagnosis was a brain tumour, one that may have been growing slowly, insidiously, for years. It was decided that the tumour was incurable, and by the end of that year, Hela was in an Auckland hospital where her siblings—my father, Czesiek, Kazik, Iza and Alina—gathered.

'Czesiek told her after the biopsy that the results were not good,' Dad says, grimacing. 'He said: "You do know you are dying, don't you, Hela?" And she looked terrified, as if she had no idea at all. She just kept looking at us all and saying, "But I don't want to die, I don't want to die. Don't let me die."'

It was the last thing Hela said before she slipped into a coma. Twenty years too late, I'm beginning to understand why my aunt's death was so painful for my father, why he is wiping tears from his cheeks with the back of his hand. Hers is the story that might have been his, the flipside of his happy-ever-after ending in this country. Hela's struggle to stay afloat, in Siberia and later New Zealand, was his struggle too. Dad's ultimate achievement, lucky or otherwise, was his ability to overcome. But in that long vigil by Hela's bedside, he had to watch his brave and determined sister doing exactly what she'd done since the Russians had thumped on their door in 1941. For the final time, and against the odds, she was fighting to stay alive.

⁓

My husband's head is dipped over the kitchen table. Opened envelopes and this morning's newspaper are spread in front of him.

James looks up at me, smiling. 'Jeremy's at karate, Lucy's doing homework. How did it go?'

'Fine, I think I've made some progress. I spoke to Geoff Bennett.'

James had left the house that morning urging me to track down the New Plymouth boy who had later written about his recollections of my teenaged father. 'Who knows,' he'd said, tucking running gear into an old zip-up bag. 'He might be waiting to hear from you.'

'But he might also be dead,' I said. 'He'd be in his 80s by now.'

'Well then you won't be able to talk to him if he's dead. But if he's alive, you will.'

James doesn't pull punches. His no-nonsense approach was one of the things that appealed to me about him when we met, barely out of university. I knew I could depend on this fair-skinned, blue-eyed son of a well-to-do fourth-generation New Zealand woman and a Scottish sea captain. James did what he said he would do, and meant what he said. Even now, after 22 years of marriage, the foggy complexities of my circular thinking still puzzle him. In our bad moments, I think he misses subtleties; he thinks I'm all over the place. When things are good, my intuition and his accountant logic travel well together. But he won't let me get away with anything woolly. Why would I wait any longer to follow up on finding this man, when both of the men involved are so old? Wasn't I curious to know more about the boy my father used to be? Wasn't this what I'd been brooding about when I'd been downstairs, unable to sleep, at three o'clock that morning?

'Just find a number and call the guy,' he'd said. 'How could it hurt? If you don't want to do it, I will.'

Geoff Bennett, I had to admit, had been surprisingly easy to track down. (It makes me think about the conversation I'd had only a few weeks ago with our oldest daughter, home from university. 'The really annoying thing about your father,' I'd said to Anna, 'isn't that he needs to tell you the best way to do things all the time. It's that he's almost always right.') Today I'd searched Geoff's name and found a recent article from a community newspaper with a photo of an elderly man at a Rotary Club art event. Mr Bennett, the caption said, once of New Plymouth, now lived in Upper Hutt.

'Is that Geoff Bennett?' I'd asked when he'd answered the phone.

'Yes, it is,' he'd replied, his voice not nearly as shaky as I'd thought it might be. 'Can I help?' And then, quickly: 'Are you selling something?'

'No, I'm not selling anything. My name is Helena Wiśniewska. I'm wondering if you recognise my surname. Do you remember my father, Stefan?'

'I don't believe it.' He paused for a moment. 'Of course I remember Stefan. Stefan Wiśniewski. You're Stefan's daughter.'

Now I can tell James he was right: it was as if Geoff Bennett had been waiting by the phone for me to ring. He'd been very happy to chat, to re-live a holiday that was almost 70 years old, the two weeks of his childhood when a sad Polish boy had come to stay.

Stefan had been very quiet when he arrived, he said. The local Taranaki Scouts had invited a number of Polish Scouts to stay with local families, an early-winter break from Pahiatua Camp life. My 15-year-old father had been the boy allotted to the Bennett household. Geoff's brother, 16-year-old Don, was the official host, but by the time the boys arrived in May 1945 Don had left school and taken on a printing apprenticeship. His younger brother, 13-year-old Geoff, had been left to entertain the Polish newcomer. Initially the boys were cautious around each other.

'My Dad had died before the war, so it was just my brother, my mother and me,' Geoff told me. 'We lived in pretty basic circumstances. I don't know what your father thought of that because he didn't say much. I suppose he knew very little English, but he loosened up after I found an old bike and we took off around the place.' But it was Stefan's attitude to Geoff's mother that made a lasting impression. 'He was so respectful towards her. In fact, I have to say there was a real dignity and sadness about your father, and it really got to me. I couldn't believe what he had been through. You've got no idea what an impact he had.'

'I'll tell him you have such nice memories of him,' I'd said. 'He'll be thrilled.'

'Oh, he's alive? Stefan's alive?' Geoff had answered. 'I thought you were ringing to tell me he'd passed away. That's wonderful news.'

When I reach this part of the story, James turns to face me. He has his hands clasped between his legs, smiling.

'So have you told your father you've spoken to him?' James asks.

Dad couldn't believe that I'd found him, I say. 'He wants to meet up with Geoff now, to invite him for lunch. He says he never got a chance to thank them properly, that it was a wonderful holiday, and that he's never forgotten it. It's something he's regretted, that he should have done before now.'

Then I stop and look more closely at James, whose eyes are reddening and pooling with tears.

'Are you crying?' I ask. 'Why are you crying?'

'I don't know,' he says, self-conscious now. 'I just think that's cool. That he wants to say thank you.'

~

He would be easy to spot, Geoff Bennett had joked on the phone with me. 'I'll be the tall, old guy,' he'd said, 'the one with a stick.'

Now, as Dad and I pull up at the railway station entrance, the place we are to meet, Geoff's standing tall as promised under the building's columns. He has a wooden stick in his right hand, a full head of silver hair carefully combed and swept neatly to one side. But I can see even from a distance that he's in poor health: his left arm is curved around his torso; his face is slumped on one side. He's several years younger than my father and looks much older. Turned away from us, looking towards the city's grey harbour, Geoff doesn't see my father until he's almost at his shoulder. I watch the two men clasp hands, smiling and searching each other's aged faces for the boys they remember. Then they hug for what seems to be a long time.

Over lunch, Geoff talks to Dad while my mother and I listen. He has 70 years of separate history, a lot to share. He tells us he has never married, and worked as a carpenter and then a hospital orderly before managing a sheltered workshop for disabled adults in Upper Hutt. He stayed involved with the Scout movement for many years.

'I didn't plan things very well. I haven't got any money now,' he says. 'But I've got a little house. And I'm very happy I've lived long enough to meet up with this man here again. You've no idea what a great day this is,' he says, looking at me.

In May 1945, my father had been in New Zealand less than a year. He was about to be moved from the relative safety of the Pahiatua camp to school in Auckland. Yes, Dad says, Geoff was right when he wrote about him on that holiday; he *was* sad. It was a period of terrible unhappiness for him. He was homesick. But he was never ungrateful. The holiday he had in New Plymouth— 'how long was it? A week? Ten days?'—was the first holiday he'd had, ever. It was also his first experience of Kiwi generosity. 'Your mother was wonderful to me, you all were,' Dad says. 'I hadn't been in a real family home, in anyone's home, since before the war. It was awful that I couldn't explain all this then.

'Do you remember the VE Day parade?' he asks now. 'While I was with you in New Plymouth?'

Allied victory in Europe was declared on May 8 that year and the Polish visitors were asked to be part of the celebrations in the city's main streets. But when Stefan was assigned a place in the parade he was given a Russian flag to wave. 'Can you believe they expected me to wave that flag? Can you believe it? I threw it on the ground. No one understood why I refused. I remember they looked at me like I'd gone mad.'

Geoff leans forward in his chair, as if making sure my father will listen to his response. 'But you know, don't you, Stefan,' he says, 'that everybody meant well. We all had the very best of intentions. We just didn't know. We had no idea.'

The two men are silent for a moment.

'Anyway, you did give me something before you left,' Geoff says. 'I didn't know what it was: a little stone. You gave it to me and I think you were saying it had come from Persia. Do you remember?'

My father is grinning. 'So that's what happened to it. I always wondered where it had gone. I gave it to you?' The stone was a small clay tablet decorated with Islamic calligraphy. My father had taken the memento—a *turbah*, I discover later—from the Shah mosque on Esfahan's huge Imam Square shortly before his mother's death. It was the only souvenir he had from Persia, something he'd hoped to be able to take back to Poland when the war was over, a curiosity to share with his reunited family. In the end, it was one of the few things that came with him to New Zealand.

I haven't heard this story before; I'd like to know what made the stone so desirable. 'Did you know what it was when you took it?' I ask.

'They used them when they were praying,' he says, 'when they bent forward, to put their foreheads on.' Then there's a pause, as if he, too, is trying to reconnect with a 14-year-old boy who'd stood in the gloom of a blue-tiled mosque with an Islamic prayer stone in his hand. What had prompted him to slip it quietly into his pocket? 'There were hundreds of them,' he says now, defensive. 'They were everywhere. No one would have noticed.'

Dad looks at Geoff. 'So, do you still have it? Did you keep the stone?' I can hear the excitement in his voice.

'No. No, it's gone. I'm sorry,' Geoff says. 'But I remember. I remember that you gave it to me.'

I wonder at the way an object so casually acquired and then forgotten can come to mean so much. I'm reminded of the piece of rubble I'd slipped into my pocket at the site of the old family home in Brest, the rough feel of it in my hand and my casual dismissal of its loss at the time. Did our driver fling it from the back seat of his Belarusian taxi later that day, an annoying piece of debris left by his strange passengers? Why was I so careless? I wish now that I'd been able to put that souvenir on my grandmother's grave in Tehran last year, a small piece of the home she'd left behind. The thought never occurred to me then. I wonder now if I'll get another chance.

It makes me think of all the people who begin somewhere and end somewhere else, gathered up like stones with the best or worst of intentions, or sometimes no intentions at all. Next to me, my own mother is still listening as a stranger tells us about the child her husband once was. She's wondering, I know, about her place in this story: what about *her* damaged family, *her* losses? When this reunion's over, Mum and I will organise a headstone for her father. I'd like to ask her nephew Darian to its unveiling, so we can talk more about the family that Mum shouldn't be ashamed of. And maybe we'll go back to the cemetery so close to our homes and place our own stones on the grave of her grandmother. I'm sure Hannah, the woman who poured coffee for Maxim Gorky, would have been a good listener too. At a table in a room by another sea, a few lifetimes ago, maybe Hannah listened quietly while her husband's dark-haired guest spoke about his bold hopes for the future. Maybe it was at her table that he spoke words he would later take home and write down.

'Everybody, my friend, everybody lives for something better to come,' Gorky might have said.

'That's why we want to be considerate of every man—who knows what's in him, why he was born and what he can do?'

~

Geoff is ready to go home now; he's getting tired. He says he'll catch a train back to Upper Hutt, but when I offer to drive him he doesn't argue.

'I'll come too,' Dad says. 'I'll keep you company.'

On the wet motorway north, conversation slows. Perhaps there's little more to be said about a 70-year-old memory, a week that two boys spent riding through Taranaki countryside together on borrowed bikes. At our destination, a wide street that stretches to a horizon of misty hills, we pull over. Drizzle is falling.

'This is me, down this drive. But don't come in,' Geoff says, 'there's nowhere to turn around. I'll be fine from here.'

He kisses my cheek and then holds Dad's hand in a long goodbye outside the car. As we pull away, I watch my father's friend in the rear vision mirror. He stoops to retrieve mail from his letterbox and stands, leaning on his stick, watching us go. I wonder if we'll see him again.

'Well that went very well,' my father says. 'I enjoyed that.'

I know these understated words reflect deep satisfaction.

He is happy, humming, turning the dial on the radio. In many ways, this has been an easy circle to help my father close: Geoff Bennett is on our doorstep, and he's happier to reminisce with us than I'd hoped. Other circles remain open. A return to Siberia—a journey I now realise with a pang that I'm eager to do—remains a challenge on a different scale. I can map in my mind the journey Dad and I should take, following the route of that cattle wagon with its terrified human cargo from Poland's east across the Urals to Siberia, perhaps travelling south into Central Asia like he did, to Uzbekistan, Turkmenistan and even across the Caspian Sea into Iran. In the relative comfort of modern Russian trains we could make wry comparisons with his original exile: the plentiful food, the helpful locals, the now passable and porous borders. We could toast his good health and our good luck with shots of vodka in the little stainless travel cups bought on our last trip to Poland; they are waiting in their leather pouch on a shelf in his Wellington kitchen for a journey just like this. Only a few years ago, Siberia would have taken just planning, money and a little nerve to set in motion. Now, as my father's 85th birthday looms, I'm afraid it will never happen.

Beyond the car, Wellington's harbour folds in on itself and the shadows of its hillsides appear and disappear behind veils of rain. Here is the same city my father woke to on a November morning in 1944, the place that's now home for us both. It's one thing to know how that journey happened for him, but it's another to understand why. The answer, if it exists, won't be found in his suitcase of yellowed photographs, or in the scent of my mother's linen cupboards. In my search, I've shaken his life from its quiet house, scattered its belongings on worn wooden floors, and demanded answers to my questions. But nothing convincing has emerged. What I have instead is a story smudged with blank fingerprints and empty footsteps, its pages patched with missing and fading memories.

I will go to Siberia one day, even if I go alone. I'd like to stand on a plateau above the wide Ob River and throw a stone or two into its depths for all the Poles who left behind something of themselves in 1941. One will be for the mothers, the real heroes: for my grandmother Stefania, whose survivor genes I am grateful for, but have never earned or deserved. Another will be for the children—those who made it, as well as those who didn't. And one will be for Hela, my aunt and namesake, who carried her impossibly heavy burdens much too far and for much too long. Who knows where those stones might travel? Some will keep moving. Others will lie where they fall.

Geoff (left) and Don Bennett (right) with their Polish billet, New Plymouth, 1945.
'He loosened up after I found an old bike and we took off around the place.'

Acknowledgements

This book has been shaped by memory as much as it has by history. My love and thanks go to my family: to Stefan and Olga Wiśniewski, who are still telling their stories and helping create mine; and to my husband James and our children, Anna, Jeremy and Lucy, who inspired me to record them. I'm grateful to my fellow travellers, Zofia Wiśniewski and Alicja Ginders, for their wise counsel and cheerleading. *Dziękuje* also to Izabela and Mietek Ptak, Alina and Bolek Wojtowicz and Czesiek Wiśniewski, who generously offered recollections, photographs and hospitality. Other aunts and uncles whose lives overlapped with mine and whose fragments of stories appear in these pages are sadly no longer here to thank: Hela and Henek Torbus, Kazik and Barbara Wiśniewski, Basia Wiśniewska, Wacek and Jasia Wiśniewski, Benek Wiśniewski, Roman Wiśniewski and Regina Wiśniewska are instead remembered with gratitude and respect.

Many friends and family will be unaware of the contribution they have made to this memoir. My mother's story would never have been explored, even to the limited extent that it has, without Darian Zam's hard work and research. I hope the cousins who grew up with me recognise the moments and the part they played in them; I'm particularly grateful to Wojtek Wiśniewski and his family, who have always offered a generous Polish welcome to visiting Kiwi relatives. Some people came for lunch and inspired chapters: thank you to Geoffrey Bennett and to Marysia Schlaadt for your roles in my family's life. Others helped in quiet but powerful ways: Anne Kelly's letterbox gift of a yellowed Penguin copy of *Post-War Polish Poetry* couldn't have been more thoughtful or timely; Victoria University's Dr Simone Gigliotti gave me an hour of her time and opened my eyes to the many journeys of displacement in 20th-century Europe.

Thanks to those who contributed to the writing process at various stages. My supervisor and teacher Chris Price, and my talented classmates from the 2013 Master of Arts in Creative Writing at Victoria University's International Institute of Modern Letters, offered feedback and encouragement at critical moments in the text's early days. And Denis and Verna Adam's generous prize allowed what had been a draft thesis suddenly seem like a book.

For their invaluable input into the finished product, many thanks to Fergus Barrowman, Ashleigh Young and Kirsten McDougall from Victoria University Press.

A note on sources

When memories and recollections were insufficient, I turned to a number of other sources for help. For background on the geopolitical forces that led to my father's deportation to Siberia and subsequent journey to Iran, *The Eagle Unbowed: Poland and Poles in the Second World War* by Halik Kochanski (2012) was particularly helpful. Historian Matthew Kelly's *Finding Poland: From Tavistock to Hruzdowa and Back Again* (2010) was similarly useful for its expert view of the events that gave rise to the deportations from Eastern Poland. For information on the Poles' experience in Iran, *Isfahan: City of Polish Children* (2001) was invaluable. Also helpful was the *Kresy-Siberia Virtual Museum*, a website established by the Kresy Siberia Foundation for 'researching, remembering and recognising the Polish citizens deported, enslaved and killed by the Soviet Union during World War Two.'

One of the earliest New Zealand books specifically relevant to the Polish diaspora in this country was Krystyna Skwarko's *The Invited* (1974), an account of one of the adult caregivers who accompanied the children to Pahiatua. This text was useful on a number of occasions, as was the more current and necessarily concise summary of that experience written by Theresa Sawicka, 'Poles', available online at Te Ara, the Encyclopaedia of New Zealand. Of the published first-person accounts from New Zealand-based survivors, a number, including the article by Geoff Bennett, can be found in *New Zealand's First Refugees: Pahiatua's Polish Children* (2004). For earlier background on the wider Polish experience in New Zealand, including the arrival of the 1944 'orphans', J. W. Pobóg-Jaworowski's *Polish Settlers in New Zealand 1876–1987* (1976) was helpful, as was I. H. Burnley's 'The Poles', published in Massey University's *Immigrants in New*

Zealand, edited by K W Thomson and A D Trilin (1970). Other academic studies provided sociological, political and cultural insight into the Polish children's experience in New Zealand. These are included in the bibliography that follows.

I thank the poets, publishers and estates for their permission to reproduce the poetry excerpts that provided a thematic framework for various chapters.

Copyright acknowledgements

Epigraph: Hafiz, 'This Place Where You Are Right Now', *The Subject Tonight is Love: Sixty Wild and Sweet Poems of Hafiz*, trans. Daniel Landinsky (New York: Penguin, 2003), 12.

Chapter 1: Wisława Szymborska, 'Hard Life with Memory', trans. Clare Cavanagh and Stanisław Barańczak, *The New York Review of Books* (8 March 2012).

Chapter 2: Aleksander Wat, 'From Persian Parables', *Post-War Polish Poetry*, ed. Czesław Miłosz (Berkeley and Los Angeles, CA: University of California Press, 1983), 20.

Chapter 3: Czesław Miłosz, 'The Porch', *New and Collected Poems 1931–2001* (London: Penguin, 2005), 38.

Chapter 4: Zbigniew Herbert, 'Our Fear', *Post-War Polish Poetry*, ed. Czesław Miłosz (Berkeley and Los Angeles, CA: University of California Press, 1983), 130.

Chapter 5: Tadeusz Różewicz, 'Leave Us Alone', *Post-War Polish Poetry*, ed. Czesław Miłosz (Berkeley and Los Angeles, CA: University of California Press, 1983), 94.

Chapter 6: Zbigniew Herbert, 'What Our Dead Do', *The New Yorker* (9 January 1998).

Czesław Miłosz, 'The Gift', *New and Collected Poems 1931–2001* (London: Penguin, 2005), 277.

Chapter 7: Hafiz, 'Ghazal 49: On Time and Times', trans. A.Z. Foreman, *Poems Found in Translation*. http://poemsintranslation. blogspot.com.

Chapter 8: Ruth Dallas, 'Letter to a Chinese Poet', *Collected Poems* (Otago University Press, 2000), 37.

Chapter 9: Zbigniew Herbert, 'From an Unwritten Theory of Dreams', trans. Alissa Valles, *New York Review of Books* (30 June 2013).

Anne Frank, *The Diary of a Young Girl* (London: Penguin, 2007), Kindle edition, entry 15 July 1944.

Vladimir Nabokov, *Speak, Memory* (New York: Vintage Books, 1989), 55.

D.H. Lawrence, *Lady Chatterley's Lover* (New York: Bantam Books, 2007), 51.

Chapter 10: Wisława Szymborska, 'Utopia', trans. S. Baranczak and C. Cavanagh, *View with a Grain of Sand: Selected Poems* (New York: Harcourt Brace and Company, 1995), 127.

Chapter 11: Leopold Staff, 'The Bridge', *Post-War Polish Poetry,* ed. Czesław Miłosz (Berkeley and Los Angeles, CA: University of California Press, 1983), 2.

Maxim Gorky, 'The Lower Depths', *Seven Plays of Maxim Gorky*, trans. Alexander Bakshy (Yale University Press, 1947), 63.

Bibliography

Beaglehole, Anne. 'Looking Back and Glancing Sideways: Refugee Policy and Multicultural Nation-Building in New Zealand'. In *Does History Matter? Making and Debating Citizenship, Immigration and Refugee Policy in Australia and New Zealand*, edited by Klaus Newman and Glenda Tavan. Canberra: ANU E Press, 2009.

Beaupré-Stankiewicz, Irena; Danuta Waszczuk-Kamieniecka; Jadwiga Lewicka-Howells; and Association of Former Pupils of Polish Schools, Isfahan and Lebanon, eds. *Isfahan: City of Polish Children*. London: Association of Former Pupils of Polish Schools, Isfahan and Lebanon, 2001.

Burnley, I.H. 'The Poles'. In *Immigrants in New Zealand*, edited by K.W. Thomson and A.D. Trlin, 125–51. Palmerston North: Massey University, 1970.

Dallas, Ruth. *Collected Poems*. Dunedin: Otago University Press, 2000.

Gorky, Maxim. *Seven Plays of Maxim Gorky*, translated by Alexander Bakshy. Yale University Press, 1947.

Hafiz. *The Subject Tonight is Love: Sixty Wild and Sweet Poems of Hafiz*, translated by Daniel Landinsky. New York: Penguin, 2003.

Kelly, Matthew. *Finding Poland: From Tavistock to Hruzdowa and Back Again*. London: Vintage Books, 2010.

Kochanski, Halik. *The Eagle Unbowed: Poland and the Poles in the Second World War*. Cambridge, MA: Harvard University Press, 2012.

Krystman-Ostrowska, Teresa Marja. *The Socio-Political Characteristics of Polish Immigration in Two New Zealand*

Communities. Master's thesis, University of Waikato, 1975.

Lawrence, D.H. *Lady Chatterley's Lover.* New York: Bantam Books, 2007.

Miłosz, Czesław, ed. *Post-War Polish Poetry.* London: Penguin, 1965. Expanded edition: Berkeley and Los Angeles, CA: University of California Press, 1983.

Miłosz, Czesław. *New and Collected Poems 1931–2001.* London: Penguin, 2005.

Nabokov, Vladimir. *Speak, Memory.* New York: Vintage Books, 1989.

Pobóg-Jaworowski, J.W. *History of the Polish Settlers in New Zealand 1776–1987.* Wellington: J.W. Pobóg-Jaworowski, 1976.

Polish Children's Reunion Committee, eds. *New Zealand's First Refugees: Pahiatua's Polish Children.* Wellington, 2004.

Sawicka, Theresa. 'Poles'. *Te Ara—the Encyclopaedia of New Zealand.* http://teara.govt.nz

Sawicka-Brockie, Theresa. *Forsaken Journeys: The Polish Experience and Identity of the 'Pahiatua Children' in New Zealand.* PhD dissertation, University of Auckland, 1987.

Skwarko, Krystyna. *The Invited: The Story of the 733 Polish Children Who Grew Up in New Zealand.* Wellington: Millwood, 1974.

Szymborska, Wisława. *View with a Grain of Sand: Selected Poems,* translated by S. Baranczak and C. Cavanagh. New York: Harcourt Brace and Company, 1995.

Tyhurst, L. 'Displacement and Migration: A Study in Social Psychiatry'. *American Journal of Psychiatry,* no. 3 (1951), 561–68.